Edward De Fonblanque

Niphon and Pe-che-li

Two years in Japan and northern China. Second Edition

Edward De Fonblanque

Niphon and Pe-che-li
Two years in Japan and northern China. Second Edition

ISBN/EAN: 9783337173852

Printed in Europe, USA, Canada, Australia, Japan

Cover: Foto ©Andreas Hilbeck / pixelio.de

More available books at **www.hansebooks.com**

Niphon and Pe-che-li;

OR,

TWO YEARS

IN

JAPAN AND NORTHERN CHINA.

BY

EDWARD BARRINGTON DE FONBLANQUE.

SECOND EDITION.

LONDON:

SAUNDERS, OTLEY, AND CO.,

66, BROOK STREET, HANOVER SQUARE.

1863.

Inscribed

TO MY WIFE.

London, 8th *April*, 1862.

NIPHON.

How much do the actions of the great influence
the lives of humble people! Because an ambassador was over-confident, and an admiral
over-rash in the north of the Chinese Empire,
the machinery was set in motion for transport-
ing 12,000 men to the scene of their blunders;
and, by the working of one of the little wheels,
I was lifted out of a happy home, dragged from
the bosom of a fond family, and shipped for the
muddy banks of the Peiho.

My kind friends owned that it was a great
bore for me; "but then," they added by way of
consolation, "we quite envy you that delightful
overland voyage, a perfect pic-nic!"

Many a time, while on board the Peninsular
and Oriental steam-ship *Nemesis*, where if you
closed your ports you were suffocated, and if you

opened them, you were drowned; where each cabin was tenanted by five more or less sea-sick passengers, with one washhand-basin between them; where everybody vied with his or her neighbour to make himself or herself as disagreeable as possible; where ladies (real ladies!—ladies of Indian officials many of them!) squabbled and fought like schoolboys for precedency at table and for berths; and even Mrs. Commissioners and Mrs. Generals lost their tempers—but never forgot their rank— many a time, I say, while suffering under all these miseries, did I feel vindictive enough to wish my consolatory friends in my place; they would never talk about pic-nics again after a three weeks' voyage in the good steam-ship *Nemesis.*

Once arrived at Ceylon, however, where the Indian passengers, with increased dignity, and a calm contempt for those destined for China, left us, we fell into better hands. Before we disembarked, Colonel Cash, whose wife had been bitten by a cock-roach in open day, wrote a round robin to the *Times,* impeaching the ship, the captain, and the Peninsular and Oriental Company. I declined to sign it, feeling no interest in the matter, and I don't know if the letter ever appeared; but if it did, it must have astonished the Company and the public.

We anchored before Hong Kong, on the 15th December, 1859; on the same date, two years later, I embarked on my return to Europe. It is of my experiences during the intervening period, passed in Japan and in the North of China, that I am about to speak.

And here I would beg my readers' attention for a minute or two, not in the old fashion, to exalt their wisdom and disparage myself, nor to ask indulgence, or acknowledge obligations, but simply to observe, that I know little or nothing of the two countries of my residence in which I intend to treat; that what knowledge I have is in all probability extremely inaccurate; that I have worked up no statistics, studied no institutions, borrowed no ideas, and discovered no secret sources of information. My little book has therefore no pretension to be instructive, or in any way useful or valuable; and those who look for such merits had better shut it up at once,* and read dear old Kaempfner or l'Abbé

* I may safely assert that there is no European living who can speak authentically on Japan ; and as regards China, the few who, by long residence and earnest study, have acquired some knowledge of that country (and such must, even in the case of the French and Russian missionaries, who have had the best opportunities of judging, be very limited) become so warped in their judgment, and so violent in their predilections or antipathies, as to incapacitate themselves from bearing true testimony.   Paradoxical as it may appear, it is the fact, that the longer a man lives in China the less capable he becomes to give information about it.   The usual effect upon an Englishman condemned to pass a large portion of his life in that country is one of disgust so unreasoning or contempt so thorough, that he loses sight of every redeeming feature, and would exterminate the race like so much vermin.   There are others who rush into the opposite extreme, and who become so absorbed in their favourite pursuit of studying China and the Chinese, as to lose sight of all English principles and modes of thought; who learn to excuse, if not to tolerate, corruption, cowardice, treachery, lying, and even worse vices, because they are "institutions," and find nothing so bad in the land of their adoption, but that they can find something worse in the land of their birth.

As a man who devotes himself to the contemplation of the planets is apt to become oblivious of the sublunary world in which he moves, so these British Chinamen, in their admiration of the Celestial Empire, forget their own origin and habits.   I can mention one eminent Chinese scholar who has so completely outlived English ideas, that if he were asked to de Huc, upon whom, by the way, all modern writers on Japan and China have mercilessly sponged for their facts. They are quite right; these gentlemen knew more about it than any of them ever will.

In a land where all men are liars (for I must admit that even my friends the Japanese are not exempt from the most prominent characteristic of Eastern nations),—and where from policy, from fear, from interest, or from habit, every native systematically conceals or misrepresents all facts bearing upon the condition of his country—it is obviously impossible for a stranger to arrive at the truth. I passed nearly a year in Japan, and the nature of my duties brought me into contact with men of all ranks and conditions, from Cabinet Ministers and governors of pro-

sketch a pretty English landscape, he would be sure to produce a scene resembling the willow pattern on our old-fashioned dinner plates. Such men are unfair representatives of English character and ideas.

The fact is, that a lengthened residence in the East warps the mental and moral, as it undermines the physical, constitution of Europeans. Of this there are too many notable examples.

vinces to horse-dealers. After three months' residence I thought I knew all that was to be known. In six months I began to have doubts as to the correctness of my knowledge, and by the time I left the country I felt that I knew nothing whatever about it.* Still there are certain things which upon the evidence of my senses I may assert to be, and these may be accepted as truth; in all else I am presenting to my readers only a record of my experiences and impressions, and in doing so I shall endeavour to steer a free course between the dry realism of blue-books, published by order of the Houses of Parliament, and the rosy tints of Captain Sherard Osborn's charming romance.

A few days after my arrival at Hong Kong, General Straubenzee determined upon despatch-

* I lately heard of a gentleman who, on the strength of a short residence at Nagasaki, lectured on Japan and the Japanese to an admiring and credulous English audience. This is just as though a Japanese, who might pass a few months in Jersey or Guernsey, should, on his return to his country, instruct his people in the institutions and customs of the British Empire.

ing me to Japan, for the purpose of reporting
upon the resources of that country, with reference to its capability of furnishing supplies for
the expeditionary army in China;—and, if practicable, procuring several thousand horses for
purposes of military transport.

The flag-officer commanding the American
squadron, Commodore Tatnall, who was about
proceeding to Japan to receive on board, for conveyance to the United States, the Japanese
Embassy, was obliging enough to offer me a
passage in the *Powhattan*, and I accordingly
proceeded to Kanagawa as his guest. It was
he, a brave and accomplished sailor and a
thorough gentleman, who, during the disastrous
affair at the mouth of the Peiho, in the preceding year, on seeing the crews of our disabled and stranded gunboats exposed to a
deadly fire, forgot every consideration but that
of humanity, and carried his ship into action
to the rescue of our sailors. Those who would
estimate this act at its true value should remember how stringent a neutrality had been
maintained by the American Government in our

disputes with China, how ostentatiously the
United States' representative had separated his
line of policy from that of his English and
French colleagues, and, above all, how great a
risk the Commodore incurred when, by a direct
breach of neutrality, he virtually made himself a
party to the war in aid of a Power of which a
large portion of the American public are always
jealous, and of whose proceedings in China, while
ever ready to profit by them, their Government
affected to disapprove.

In the course of this noble act his boatswain
was unfortunately killed by his side. Here was a
terrible aggravation of his guilt; the blood of
an American citizen shed to gratify the British
predilections of the insubordinate Commodore!
Here was matter for the New York papers!
What could forty years of gallant and devoted
service count against such enormity?

The Commodore was still, at the time I was
on board the *Powhattan*, ignorant of what view
the Government would take of his conduct.
The outcry on the part of a large portion of
the press was violent, and the general im-

pression was that it would go hard with him.
He thought so himself :—

"I committed a direct breach of orders," he
said to me, in allusion to this affair, "but when
I saw your fine fellows helpless under that fire,
it was more than flesh and blood could stand;
I would do the same again, though they dis-
missed me for it."

It was with sincere pleasure that on reaching
Japan I heard from this noble old man that he
had found despatches awaiting him, in which
the President had expressed his approval of the
course adopted; and although this was conveyed in the very driest official language, it cannot be doubted that the humanity and gallantry
of Commodore Tatnall was fully appreciated by
the better, if not by the larger number, of his
countrymen.

We had an agreeable passage; everything on
board appeared to me to be conducted with
perfect order and regularity, although I missed
the smartness and cleanliness of an English
man-of-war, as also the light-heartedness and
gaiety of our own sailors. Nothing could

exceed the kindness of the officers. One of them, Lieutenant Habersham, is the author of an excellent work on Japan,* which he visited while attached to Commodore Perry's expedition, and which so completely won his heart, that on our arrival he resigned his commission, and established himself as a merchant at Yohuhama. If intelligence and energy can make a man's fortune in Japan, he ought to become a millionaire. Another has recently acquired fame as the Commander of the Confederate steamer *Nashville.*

We sailed from Hong Kong on the 31st December, and I assisted in drinking out the old year under the shadow of the stars and stripes. On the 8th January we passed a group of volcanic islands, some of them in full eruption. I asked one of the sailors who had been employed on a survey in these seas what the volcanoes were called. He looked at me with that peculiar air of mingled shrewdness and simplicity which an American puts on when saying a smart thing to a stranger, and, turning

* " A North Pacific Exploring Expedition."

the quid in his cheek, replied deliberately, " Wall, I don't know how it's called, but I guess it *smells* more like hell than anything *I* ever smelt ! "

On the 10th we caught the first glimpse of the snowy peak of Fusi-jama sparkling in the morning sun ; and on the following day, after skirting a lovely bit of sea-coast (lovely even in the midst of winter, with the thermometer at 28 degrees, and a snow-storm blowing), we dropped anchor in the fair Bay of Kanagawa.

We were immediately boarded by a boat-load of officials, who looked, to my inexperienced eyes, more unlike men than any human males I ever beheld ; their flowing robes, petticoat trowsers, and bandaged noses, giving them rather the appearance of old applewomen at their stalls on a cold day than of government officers. They wore two swords, by which at first sight they appeared to be transfixed through their bodies ; on closer inspection, however, I satisfied myself that they were not skewered, but that the weapons were only stuck through their girdles at an acute angle.

When they took off their hats and untied their
noses, the superiority of their features and
expressions over those of the Chinese was very
noticeable.

They were accompanied by an interpreter, a
remarkably handsome boy, who was evidently
very proud of his English, which consisted in
" How do you do?" and "I say," of which he
made the most; he spoke Dutch very fluently
however.

I lost no time in landing at Kanagawa, and
proceeded, the observed of all observers—for at
that time Europeans were still wonders in these
parts—and assailed by volleys of "Ohios," (which
I was glad to learn had no reference to the
American flag under which I had sailed, but
signified "welcome,") to the British Consulate,
where Captain Howard Vyse, some time of the
B Troop of Her Majesty's Horse Guards Blue,
provided me with a pony and an interpreter to
make my way to Yedo, a distance of about
eighteen miles. The road, which for the greater
part skirts the sea, is wide, and in admirable
repair; houses, small settlements, or consider-

able villages, flank it nearly the whole way, so as to give the approach to the capital the appearance of a long, straggling suburb. Wherever there are no buildings large trees are planted on each side of the road, and on the land side stretch extensive rice fields, bounded by green hills.

The village of Kavasaki, on the river Logo, and about half-way between Kanagawa and Yedo, is the boundary, which under the treaty no foreigner can pass unless provided with a passport from his Minister. We were here stopped accordingly by a benevolent-looking old "Yaconin,"* who emerged from a kind of guard-house on the bank, carrying a fan and wearing his two swords in a very determined fashion. Having satisfied him of our right to pass, he ordered boats to ferry us and our horses across the river, and, with a courteous salutation, re-entered his den.

While preparing to cross the stream, which is here broad, deep, and rapid, we partook of tea,

---

* The term Yaconin is applicable to all classes of government *employés* above or below a certain rank.

which a bevy of damsels from an adjoining
house of entertainment forced upon us. Prepared as I had been by Sherard Osborn for
meeting with great beauty among the Japanese
women, I must own to some surprise at the
entire absence of anything like good looks
among these tea-house girls, who, with coarsely-
painted faces, very elaborate head-dresses, be-
dizened with tinsel, stamping clumsily on wooden
pattens, in petticoats so narrow as to impede
their walking, surrounded us, holding out little
tiny egg-shell cups on lacquer trays, and " Ohio-
ing " vociferously. The Japanese tea has a
peculiar but very delicate flavour, which gains
upon one, and drunk, of course, without the
artificial accompaniments of milk and sugar,
out of the thinnest possible porcelain, was very
grateful. All along the road we met with this
attention; at every tea-house—and they are
plentiful—men rushed out with pails to water
our horses, and women with tea, sweetmeats,
and the fire-box; both always with a kindly smile
and a display of the most brilliant teeth that
ever a race was blest with. As we rode on, we

were followed by a storm of " Sionadas" (farewell), and now and then a little child would scamper off in alarm, crying out " Tojee, Tojee ! " (a somewhat reproachful term, applied indiscriminately to all foreigners,) changing the note to " Ohio " after we, and its alarm, had passed. The impression conveyed to me by my first ride in Japan was that the country people are extremely friendly, and by no means ill-disposed to intercourse with foreigners.

It was towards dusk that we entered Sinagawa, the long suburb of Yedo, a little beyond the termination of which the Legation is situated. Here the character of the people changed; no Ohios greeted us; the shopkeepers stared at us from their doorways with mingled curiosity and impudence; officials strolled or rode past us with unconcealed disdain in their looks, and fine sturdily-built men, with the independent upright carriage of a race accustomed to bear and to use arms, swaggered and sometimes reeled by us with a defiant and insolent air, and occasionally the utterance of a gesture or a salutation more expressive than polite.

These are the Daimio's followers; the swash-bucklers of our own baronial times reproduced in an Eastern form; fellows without social ties or moral obligations, ready to cut you in half on the slightest provocation, and as ready to commit the Hari Kari upon themselves at the command of their chief.

Sinagawa is filled with houses of entertainment to which the Daimio's followers resort, and where they pass whole days, or as long as their money will last, in drinking, gambling, and dissipation of all kinds. It would be certain death for an European to enter one of those dens, and even the open streets are unsafe for him after dark.

Two fellows, who had evidently partaken freely of *saki*, placed themselves directly in our path, and, grasping their sword hilts, looking full in our faces, saluted us with the word "Baca," which means much the same as the forbidden "Raca" of the Scriptures. My companion laid his hand ostentatiously upon his holsters, and our friends, who, like all Japanese, appeared to have a wholesome horror of fire-arms, sheered off with a muttered growl.

It was now getting dark; the number of drunken revellers was increasing, and it was a relief to me when, after emerging from the narrow streets of Sinagawa, we gained an open space, bordered on one side by the blue Bay, and on the other by the park-like grounds of a Daimio's residence, and shortly after beheld the English colours flying at the head of the fine avenue leading to Tosenjee, the temple allotted as residence to the British Minister.

Mr. Alcock, our representative in Japan, was a little startled when I first made known to him the object of my mission, and foresaw many obstacles to its successful accomplishment. Sensible, however, of the importance, both in a military and economical point of view, of obtaining in Japan a large supply of transport animals, for service at the seat of the coming war in China, he promised me his cordial support, and this he never, from first to last, failed to afford me. He lost no time in applying for an interview with the Minister for Foreign Affairs on the subject, and this being appointed, I had a couple of days at my disposal for seeing the capital.

Apart from the gratification of curiosity in visiting a city from which Europeans had been excluded for centuries, and which even now is so rarely visited,* there is much in Yedo to excite wonder and admiration. What first strikes us, as an unusual feature in Eastern cities, is the admirable order and cleanliness of the town, its broad, well-paved streets, handsome shops, and the prosperous appearance of its crowded population. The main street, which may be said to begin where the suburb of Sinagawa ends, appears interminable, and is probably not less than eight miles in length. At about each quarter of a mile there is a barrier and guard-house, in appearance like one of our turnpikes, presided over by a Yaconin and an armed party, whose duty it is, on the first symptoms of any popular commotion, on the committal of a crime, or the out-

* Under the terms of the Treaty, Yedo should be opened to foreign traders in 1862. As, however, it offers few advantages to commerce, and the danger of collision with the natives in a densely-crowded capital is so imminent, it is to be hoped that an equivalent, for what must necessarily outrage national prejudices and affords but doubtful benefit, will be accepted on the part of the Treaty Powers.

break of a fire, to close his gates, and sound
a signal of alarm, whereupon similar precautions
are at once adopted in all the adjoining districts
of the city. By this means, large gatherings of
people are prevented, and the capture of offenders
against the laws is greatly facilitated. I remember once deriving the benefit of these barriers,
when, in an attempt to " do some shopping " in
Yedo on foot, in company with a naval officer,
the Yaconins on duty invariably closed their
gates immediately behind us, to shut out and
prevent our being annoyed by the dense crowds
which dogged our steps.

The most striking part of Yedo is undoubtedly the official quarter, in which the Tycoon's
Palace, the principal government establishments,
and the palaces of the Daimios, are situated.
The former is an imposing edifice, of considerable
extent, standing in richly-wooded, ornamented
grounds, and surrounded by high and massive
granite walls, and a triple moat. This is the
palace, the prison, and the grave of the Tycoon.
Within these precincts he passes his splendid
and miserable life. Raised by the misfortune

of his rank above all other men, he is excluded
from their pleasures, their trials, and their sympathies. Here kneeling princes offer him their
lip service, and flattering courtiers minister to
his wants; but how often must he wish himself a common mortal! how wearily must he
yearn for that bright world beyond his prison
walls, for the pure air of those green mountains, and the fresh breezes of the blue sea; * so
near, ever so near, yet so hopelessly beyond his
reach! "Uneasy lies the head that wears a
crown" all the world over, and in all lands are
rulers compelled to make some personal sacri-
fices in return for the power they wield; but
the poor Tycoon is only a sovereign in name;
all the magnificent pains and penalties of greatness are his to an extent unparalleled elsewhere;
but he has less power for good or evil than the
least of the turbulent Daimios who kneels before
his throne; and ostensibly the head and the

* How his courtiers must have chuckled when Lord Elgin,
in the name of the Queen of England, presented the Tycoon
with a yacht! What would the Cardinals say if the Sultan
were to select the most lovely of his harem and send her to
the Pope for a wife?

leader of his subject princes, he is in fact, throughout his reign, by turns, their tool, their slave, and their victim.*   Debarred from all that can cheer, refine, or elevate a man, he drags through life his golden chain, more lonely and more hopeless, with less in the past to console, and less in the future to cheer him, than the meanest Yaconin lounging among the guard at his palace gate.

The present Tycoon is but a boy of eighteen —very fat and scorbutic for his age.   Mr. Townshend Harris, the United States Minister, was the first foreigner ever admitted to an audience with a Tycoon ; and the Japanese looked upon him as a wonder accordingly, saying : " Behold, there is a Tojin whose eyes have beheld the Tycoon, and he lives ! "   Mr. Alcock, subsequently, ventured into the presence, and not only survived it, but was treated with so much greater courtesy than his colleague (who

---

* The Tycoon's influence in the Great Council of State, over which he presides, does not probably exceed that of the Speaker in our House of Commons; he is, in fact, in name the first Daimio, as the other is in name the first Commoner.

it is to be feared was terribly snubbed), that the latter insisted upon a second and more flattering reception. I do not know if he ever got it.

On the occasion of Mr. Alcock's interview, however, in order to conceal its true nature from the public, lest so glaring a concession to foreigners should give rise to scandal, the courtiers and officials in attendance wore yellow robes—this being the costume prescribed by court etiquette on occasions of tribute offered by subject Powers;* and no doubt the general impression prevailed in Yedo that the British Envoy had been graciously permitted to lay Queen Victoria's humble submission at the Tycoon's feet.

It is evident that the palace in Yedo was not built without keeping in view the possibility of its being attacked; and it would be no easy matter to take it by assault, though there are some heights conveniently situated for bombarding it.

---

* *En revanche*, however, Mr. Alcock had obtained the great concession of being admitted to the presence without " kowtowing," or the performance of any marks of respect beyond those usual at our own Court.

The outer walls are massive and well constructed, and, as is usual in Japan, built entirely without cement; being composed of huge blocks of granite so cut into various forms, regular and irregular, as to fit one into the other with such perfect nicety that it would be difficult to insert the blade of a knife between any two of them. This plan is adopted, not from the want of cement or mortar, of which there are several excellent kinds, but to guard against earthquakes, which make, they say, less impression upon a yielding than a solid mass.

Many of the Daimios' residences stand within their own grounds, almost hidden from view by dense masses of magnificent timber; among which the cedar and maple predominate. Others, covering an area of a square quarter mile, present outwardly the appearance of solidly-built barracks, which in fact they are—for it is said that the Daimios, during their residence in Yedo,* bring a large proportion of their fol-

* Every Daimio is required to pass six months of each year in the capital, and by way of furnishing further security for his good conduct while absent from Court, must leave his

lowers with them, and some are reported to harbour no less than 20,000 men within the walls of their palaces in the capital.

The size of Yedo consists chiefly in its length,—I do not think that in depth the city exceeds three miles; and having once turned off at a right angle from the main street we plunged almost suddenly from the bustle, crowd, and noise of a capital into the perfect stillness of a lovely country landscape. Turning to look from the height above the Tycoon's Palace, we had an excellent view of the city, running along north and south, and presenting one dense mass of house-tops as far as the eye could stretch. A minute more and we were riding in quiet green lanes—between hedges of camelias, nectarine, peach-blossoms, and jessamine, which, in spite of a frosty atmosphere, for the thermometer stood at 22 degrees, burst forth in bud and blossom to greet the bright, warm sun. It was my first country ride in Japan, and I can-

wives and children behind him on his return to his own dominions. How his domestic happiness is provided for during one-half of his life does not appear.

not forget how deeply I was impressed with the beauty of the country and its wondrous richness of vegetation; yet the character of the scenery around Yedo is by no means striking or peculiar, in comparison with other parts of Japan, and bears some resemblance to a quiet English country landscape, when beheld at its best season and in its brightest colours.

Extract from my Journal, Jan. 13.—This was the day fixed for my interview with the Foreign Minister, and at 10 o'clock our *cortège* left Tosenjee for the palace, within the outer walls of which the great offices of Government are situated. On occasions of this kind it is contrary to etiquette either to walk or ride, and Mr. Alcock, who makes it a point never to offend Japanese prejudices, when he loses nothing in dignity or self-respect by yielding to them, or unnecessarily to commit what to them would appear a breach of good manners, or a want of respect, adopted the very uncomfortable custom of being conveyed in *norrimons,* or chairs, suited in size to the station of the occupant, so that he either sits upright, reclines, lounges, or lies at full stretch according to his rank.*

The distance from the Legation to the Minister's could not be less. than five miles, and we were two hours in accomplishing it. Mr. Alcock in a full-length norrimon was at the head of the procession; four officers marched on each side of him, and he was preceded by 20 Yaconins, at whose head again marched two officials, who, keeping up a clatter by means of a number of iron rings hanging on a pole, cleared the road before them and warned the mob to " make way for the great man who comes." It needs no further persuasion, and the dense crowds that fill the streets form themselves into a solid wall on each side of the broad pavement, from whence in dead silence they peer and gape at the Tojins. Marching in front of Mr. Alcock his own attendants bear the Japanese insignia belonging to a rank corresponding with his; among others

* All these matters are regulated by statute, and even the pole upon which the norrimon is hung indicates distinctly by its length and the extent of its curve the rank of the owner.

a huge halbert in a sheath, and an instrument
resembling an exaggerated artillery sponging-
rod. Another carries the English colours. In
rear of his chair, and immediately before mine,
which is smaller, and in which, buttoned up to
the chin, in full uniform, with a plumed cocked
hat on my head, and spurs on my heels, I can
neither sit nor lie down, six Yaconins swagger,
armed to the teeth; two more are on each side,
and four behind me. The chair of the interpreter,
followed by a considerable guard, brings up the
rear. And thus we proceed slowly, wearily, and
very cold along the interminable streets and
through uninterrupted lines of wondering men,
women, and children, who seem in doubt whether
to prostrate themselves before the well-known
emblems of authority, or to stand erect in de-
fiance of the foreigners. They probably know
that the latter would be more agreeable to the
Yaconins in attendance; at any rate, few performed even the common obeisance habitually
made by the lower classes to the smallest
officials.

Arrived at the outer moat of the palace, which

communicates with the main gate by a well
and solidly-constructed drawbridge, our procession halted, and we were requested to descend
from our chairs. Mr. Alcock, however, as it
appears, was quite prepared for this attempt to
lower his dignity in the opinion of the Japanese
public, and insisted upon our being carried to
the very entrance of the Foreign Minister's reception-hall. On went our bearers accordingly,
over the bridge and through a spacious and
scrupulously clean court-yard, where we alighted.
A number of officials were in attendance to receive us, and ushered us through a long corridor
covered with thick matting,* of a fine texture,
into the reception-hall.

This is a well-proportioned room, of con-

---

* The Japanese find it hard to forgive Europeans for
walking in their boots over the matting which they only
tread in their stocking feet. It is in their eyes as great an
outrage as it would be in ours if a guest were to walk about
on the tablecloth at our dinner, leaving his mark at every
step. Yet there is no help for it, and this the shopkeepers
have begun to discover, for they frequently lay strips of cotton
or some other coarse covering over their mats to preserve
them from the foreigner's foot.

siderable dimensions; the wainscoating panels and window-frames are of a highly-polished black lacquer, and the walls covered with a very delicate paper, artistically painted with birds and flowers. The furniture consists of a row of small lacquer tables and chairs, placed at intervals of a few yards; and beside each, there is a large bronze urn, of ornamental design, filled with symmetrically-shaped pieces of charcoal in full glow. On each table is a similar urn, of small size, used for the double purpose of lighting pipes and warming hands.

Simplicity in furniture, as in dress, is, I am told, universal in Japan; and it appears to me, combined as it is with an artistic taste and scrupulous cleanliness, an unmistakable mark of refinement and civilization.

As I entered with Mr. Alcock at one door, the Minister approached from an opposite one, and after bowing, much in European fashion, only with a good deal more posterior protrusion, motioned us to our seats, and at the same time placed himself on the side immediately opposite, leaving an open space of about five yards between us, which was occupied by three or four men squatted in single file, on all-fours, with their foreheads touching the ground; these were the interpreters. By the side, but a little in rear of the Minister, sat two officials of rank, and behind and around these some dozen others, the governors of provinces or districts. Here and there, men holding rolls of paper, and with their writing-cases beside them, knelt on the ground. These are the scribes, who would record our proceedings.

The Foreign Minister is a middle-sized man, of moderate stature, with an open and decidedly intelligent countenance, and bright, rather restless eyes. He wore the usual flowing robes, of a sober grey-coloured silk, and the fine folds of pure white linen or crape underneath, which formed his "underclothes," indicate his rank. The dress of the others differed but little from his; but I noticed that the wide petticoat trowsers of some of these were richly brocaded in gold and colours. Of course there are dandies in Japan, as elsewhere. All wore badges upon their sleeves; these are their coats of arms or crests, or, in the

čase of inferiors, the crest of the Daimio or
other masters in whose service they are. All,
with the exception of the servants, wore two
swords.

The proceedings opened by a few words in a
low tone from the Minister. His chief interpreter — a handsome, bright-eyed man, named
Muri-Yama (the same who officiated on the occasion of Lord Elgin's visit)—inclined his head,
still bowed, as if better to catch the great man's
voice, and having struck his forehead two or
three times against the ground, turned, still
kneeling, but with head erect, and looking him
full in the face, to Mr. Alcock. I could not but
admire the clever transition, from abject submission, while communicating with his chief, to
comparative independence—still far from disrespect or familiarity—when addressing the
foreigner ; this demeanour is of course according
to regulation.

Muri-Yama loq. in Dutch.—His Highness in-
forms the English Minister that the day is cold.

Mr. Alcock's Dutch Interpreter.—He says it's
very cold, sir.

Mr. Alcock (with a shiver).—There is no doubt of it.

Dutch Interpreter.—His Excellency says that it is very cold, and hopes his Highness is well.

Muri-Yama (knocking his head thrice).—Your slave speaks not his own words but the words of the English Minister, who says that the words of your Highness are words of truth and wisdom. The English Minister also desires your slave to express his great happiness at the good health which your Highness enjoys (three knocks, and down charge).

The Minister graciously bends his head in acknowledgment of kind inquiries, and hopes Mr. Alcock is in good health. The message is conveyed through the same filtering process, and the day would probably pass in an interchange of unmeaning compliments did not Mr. Alcock bluntly propose that they should proceed to business. Several minor matters are referred to, to the evident gratification of the Foreign Minister, who receives Mr. Alcock's congratulations on the good dispositions of the Japanese Government with a gracious smile ; and having thus got him

into a good humour, our diplomatist proceeds to
open the real business of the day by stating, in a
few words—much to the point—that the Queen's
Government being in want of some horses in
China had sent over an officer (pointing to me,
whereupon I receive a bow) to purchase out of
the superabundance of Japan, and that he trusted
that the Government would afford Her Majesty's
officer every assistance in the performance of his
duty.

As the Dutch interpreter delivers this message,
Muri-Yama, who is evidently perplexed at its
nature, becomes more attentive ; at the word
" Parde," he interrupts the speaker by asking,
" Did you say horses ? " Between each sentence
he blows upon his closed fingers, and utters a
subdued "*Hein, Hein,*" and at its conclusion, nods
in token of comprehension, and proceeds in the
usual manner to convey the message to his
Chief.

The Minister listens throughout with an im-
perturbable countenance, but, as Muri-Yama
proceeds, there are looks of surprise and interest
among the lesser officials, and on many faces a

D

perplexed " What next ? " kind of expression ;
the writers are now scribbling away furiously.

A conversation in a low tone takes place before
the Minister replies. In the meantime servants
hand round tea and pipes, and as cigars are not
prohibited, and every means of warmth is most
grateful, I light my Manilla.

After a while, the Minister intimates that he
would be delighted to oblige us, but——

Mr. Alcock had led me to be prepared for many
objections being raised to my request, but thought
that, with one exception, these might be overcome.
If the Japanese Government chose to plead, that
in providing us with horses to be used for military
purposes in our war against the Chinese, they
would commit a breach of neutrality, and might
involve themselves in war, there was no answer
to their argument, and my mission was at an end.
I dreaded to hear Muri-Yama announce that this
was the view taken by the Minister; to my relief,
however, the "but" was of a less serious nature ;
there was, it was alleged, only a sufficient
number of horses in Japan to supply the wants
of the people.

This objection being quietly pooh-pooh'd, it
was inquired how many horses we wanted, and
on three or four thousand being named, there
was a buzz of surprise, and all faces but that
of the Minister, who preserved complete equanimity, expressed intense enjoyment of what
appeared to be taken for a good joke.

The discussion lasted for nearly three hours.
Many were the puerile objections raised and disposed of with perfect temper and patience on
both sides. The only unanswerable argument,
namely, that it would not become the Japanese
Government to provide us with the means of
making war upon a friendly nation, did not seem
to occur to the Minister, who at length promised
that he would endeavour to let me be provided
with one thousand horses from Niphon, and as
many more from each of the other two islands;
and with this undertaking we had to rest satisfied.

I forgot to mention that, during the discussion, we were served with luncheon composed of
excellent soup, boiled fish, and sweetmeats, accompanied by tiny cups of *Saki*. The audience

concluded, the Minister rose, made a low bow to
Mr. Alcock, another less low to me, and a third,
barely more than an inclination, to the interpreter; we respectfully returned the salutation,
and, amid a volley of prostrations and head-
knockings, left the apartment by one door as he
retired by another. Arrived in the corridor, the
governors and other officials relaxed from the
dignity of office so far as to crowd and chatter
around us. The interpreter presented me to
several of them, and the introduction em-
boldened them to proceed to a very close inspection of my dress, examining each article, and
asking questions as to its use, material, and cost.
One of them looked at my Crimean medal,
counted the clasps attached to it, and told me,
through the interpreter of course, that he saw I
had been in three actions during the war with
Russia; adding that he had heard of Sevastopol,
which we had taken after a year's fighting, and
had been obliged to give up a few days later.
My box spurs excited great admiration: I had
to take one out of its socket to show how it was
affixed to the boot, and I have no doubt—so

imitative are these Japanese—that ere long Maxwell's spurs and boxes will be an article of manufacture in Yedo.

January 14.—This morning was devoted to making purchases. As it is not expedient, or indeed, as I am told, practicable for foreigners to visit the shops in Yedo, Mr. Alcock kindly allows his entrance hall to be converted into a temporary bazaar for the benefit of his visitors; and notice having been sent yesterday, I found, on getting up this morning, a large collection of curious and beautiful specimens of Japanese ware displayed for my edification. I hardly know what I admire most : the lacquer which I found in every form, from huge unwieldy cabinets like a chest of drawers with folding doors, to tiny little toilet boxes of the most delicate make, or the porcelain—unrivalled in its way—or the quaint ivory carvings illustrative of Japanese character and habits, or the bronzes—the metal of the best of which is marvellous, and has that true ring which is sweet music to the ear of a connoisseur. I am advised not to be in a hurry in making purchases, as my taste must necessarily be unformed and requires cultivation, but there were some gems which proved too tempting for me, and after a few hours' contemplation and study of their beauties, I found myself plus a considerable number of packages (the outer cases alone are wonderfully fashioned, and their lids fit with a nicety unknown to us), and minus the sum of—never mind how much!

Of course the Japanese dealers ask a great deal more than they will take for their wares, and they appear to be indifferent arithmeticians, never making the most simple calculation without the aid of their numeral tables—a frame inclosing wires upon which little balls are strung—and even by these means they are puzzled to effect combinations. A member of the Legation told me that he had frequently obtained several articles at a cheaper price than the dealers would consent to take for one of them by itself.*

* I subsequently experienced this, and dealers, after having concluded a bargain with me and left the house, frequently

My dollars are of little use here. It appears that the Japanese Government is required, under the terms of the Treaty, to furnish each European with native money to the extent of about £2 a-day, in exchange for silver dollars, at a fixed rate;* and they further provide a limited supply of native coin for the public expenditure of officials. The itseboo, which, with its halves and quarters, forms the principal circulating medium, is an oblong silver coin inscribed with Japanese characters, and it is wonderful how neatly and compactly one hundred of these are packed in a small paper parcel. The paper of Japan, by the way, is not the least curious of the many curious things seen in this land; it has almost the tenacity of linen, and is used for many purposes besides writing upon

returned to say that they had made a mistake. Of course these errors were always against them; they never complained of having received too much.

* 311 itseboos for 100 dollars was the standard rate of exchange, but in ordinary transactions the dollar was calculated at three itseboos. It was never, however, taken willingly even at that rate, and on the exchange ceasing in June, 1860, the dollar became so depreciated that it was not always possible to obtain two itseboos for it.

and packing. Among others, it forms the substitute of glass in windows, and all ranks employ it for pocket-handkerchiefs — the patterns of some of these are really very pretty and lacelike —and the Japanese affect some disgust at our habit of retaining a "nose-cloth" about our persons after having used it.

Finding that it would not be possible for me to carry on my duties, and to form the necessary establishments for the collection and maintenance of horses in Yedo, it was arranged that I should make Kanagawa my head-quarters, visiting the capital whenever communication with Mr. Alcock, or other authorities, might require my presence.

It was very tantalizing to a lover of sport, to see, as we did during our ride to Kanagawa, innumerable wild geese and ducks feeding unconcernedly in the adjoining rice-fields, and within a few yards of our horses' feet, with a confidence in their personal safety which speaks volumes for the respect for the law prevailing in Japan. No native dare, on pain of death, fire a shot within 30 ris* of Yedo, and foreigners may not infringe this regulation. In the very heart of Yedo and its dense population, in the moats surrounding the Tycoon's Palace, thousands upon thousands of ducks and teal disport themselves in public, with a most provoking consciousness of perfect immunity from danger.

Arrived at Kavasaki, we left our horses at the tea-house before described, and proceeded to visit the Temple of Dycee, a very fair specimen of church architecture in Japan. A high-priest, dressed in gorgeous and gaudy robes, was in the act of performing service, and what with his bobbings and genuflexions, the odours of incense, the lighted tapers, the glittering ornaments, and the tinsel decorations, I could almost fancy myself in a Roman Catholic Chapel.

Shortly after my return to Kanagawa, where, thanks to the kindness of Captain Howard Vyse, I established myself at the Consulate, I went on board the *Powhattan*, where I found the principal members of the Japanese Embassy to Washing-

* About 100 English miles.

ton, inspecting their future accommodation. They were all in high good-humour, which was accounted for by the *débris* of a collation (including several very clean ham bones—ham is a very favourite dish of the Japanese), and a small regiment of empty champagne bottles. Those Japanese are certainly fond of good living, though somewhat indiscriminate in their eating and drinking, mixing soup, pastry, meat, and custards, beer, champagne and curaçoa, in a way that few Europeans' digestions or appetites could submit to. They have a curious custom, too, of pocketing what they do not eat; and the robes of the ambassadorial attendants on board the *Powhattan* bulged in all directions, from the innumerable paper parcels filled with every description of food, from boiled carrots and curry to legs of fowls and cheesecakes.

We are told a story of a boy, who, on being asked after a Christmas dinner why he was crying, complained of being unable to eat any more, and on his mamma suggesting that he should fill his pockets, sobbed out in a fresh burst of tears, that his pockets were full already.

This was a greedy little boy, and in England it is naughty to be greedy; but in Japan it is an act of politeness to eat to repletion of everything that is offered, and to carry away in one's pockets and clothes, whatever surplus food the stomach cannot contain.*

Kanagawa was originally intended to be the European trading port of Yedo; owing, however, to its obvious inferiority, for purposes of commerce, to Yokuhama—a village about three miles to the south-west—the latter became the resort of the merchants, while the Consuls alone took up their residence in temples† allotted to them in Kanagawa, which is prettily situated on the high and richly-wooded banks of the harbour, while Yokuhama is little more than a swamp recently reclaimed from the sea. But European —or I should say Anglo-Saxon—enterprise (for the great majority of the merchants were either English or American) has already worked won-

* In China it is even worse; for there, the greatest compliment a man can pay his host after dinner, is to eructate aloud, in token of his being as full as he can hold.

† Since then, all the Consulates have been removed to Yokuhama.

ders within the six months that the port has been opened ; the buildings, it is true, were of a very temporary nature, but they sufficed to house the merchant and to store his goods. The ·harbour, in which so short a time ago no foreign flag had ever been seen, was full of shipping. The wharfs were crowded with goods, and troops of coolies carrying bales and barrels on their bamboo poles, gave the place as business-like an appearance as you would notice in the old-established marts of Shanghae or Hong Kong. The Japanese had not been backward in supplying the wants of their new customers. A handsome, spacious, and solidly-built Treasury and Custom-house—a couple of stone wharfs, a well-constructed canal—and whole streets and blocks of shops, in which every description of Japanese ware was displayed, testified their readiness to " reciprocate " with the foreigners. Nor were business wants alone consulted, for the Government had considerately provided a magnificent building, all lacquer and carving and delicate painting, in which the *Tojins* might pass their leisure hours in the company of painted *moosmes,* dressed in gorgeous robes and *coiffées* in the most wonderful manner.

I visited the " Gankeroo," taking the precaution to go there in broad day, and, for my character's sake, in good company, and was a little startled at the systematic way in which the authorities conduct this establishment. Two officers showed us over the building, and pointed out its beauties with as much pride as if they were exhibiting an ancient temple sacred to their dearest gods. *This* was the court-yard; —*that* was to be a fish-pond with fountains (the building was still incomplete at this time); in this room refreshments might be procured— *that* was the theatre; *those* little nooks into which you entered by a sliding panel in the wall were dormitories, encumbered with no unnecessary furniture; *there*, affixed to the walls, was the tariff of charges, which I leave to the imagination; and in that house, across the court, seated in rows on the verandah, were the moosmes themselves. Would we step over, for it was only under male escort that they might enter the main building? My curiosity had,

however, been sufficiently gratified, and I departed, quite ready to believe in anything that
I might hear as to the morals of the Japanese.
I believe that the Government derives a considerable revenue from the Gankeroo, much as
certain Grand Dukes in Germany do from their
gaming-houses, and probably with about the
same benefit to morality.

On the principle that seeing is believing, which,
indeed, is nowhere more true than in Japan, I also
visited the public bath-houses. All that I had
heard on this subject proved to be perfectly
true; there were men, women, and children of
all ages, and in complete nudity, performing
their ablutions in common, and as little dis-
composed by the entrance of several foreigners as
by one another. They all appeared to me simply
unconscious of shame. Nor is this gross im-
modesty confined to public places; for frequently
during my rides, on the cry of " Tojin " being
raised, have I seen men and women rush stark
naked from their houses—I suppose out of their
common tub—and stand before their doorways
to gaze after me. Yet these people were pro-

bably what we should call "highly respectable,"
paying their church dues and their tradesmen's
bills with irreproachable regularity, and perhaps
even "keeping a chair."

The Japanese shops at Yokuhama, although
making a brilliant display, do not contain articles
of such value as those offered for sale in Yedo.
Occasionally a rare bit of real old lacquer, or an
antique vase, or a curious bronze, may be discovered, but as a rule the shops are filled with
articles manufactured for the European market;
and flimsily-made, gaudily-painted cabinets,—
none of your stupid knick-nacks, but a thing
that will make a show in a room,—a regular solid lump of shining furniture — find a
ready sale among trading ship-captains *et id
genus*, and not unfrequently reach England before falling to pieces, or casting their lacquer
skin.

Once you have educated your taste—and to any
man of a cultivated mind this is a natural process—you cannot tolerate the trashy productions
foisted upon foreigners as Japan ware, and could
no more mistake the veritable old lacquer,

bronzes, ivory carvings, or porcelain for the modern imitations than you would confound a head by Rembrandt with a portrait by Désanges. Whether it be that the secret of the manufacture of the best lacquer is extinct, or that it absolutely requires age to perfect it, certain it is that such specimens are rare, and I believe it is only the necessities of impoverished nobles and gentlemen (who are the great collectors) that ever brings them into the market, where they have as intrinsic a value as a diamond has in Europe. The best specimens I have—out of a rather good collection—are presents given to me as souvenirs on my leaving Japan by native officials. Upon these few people in England would bestow much attention, but they are perfect works of art of an Eastern pre-Raphaelite school, and the more minutely they are inspected the more admirable they appear. Some of them indeed require the aid of a microscope to do their beauties full justice.

Old porcelain is extremely rare in Japan, but so highly valued that I have been assured that as much as 500 itseboos (about £40) has

frequently been offered for a fragment to replace
an absent piece in an ancient cup or plate. The
egg-shell and jewelled china, so much and so
justly admired, is all of modern manufacture,
and the demand for it within the last two or
three years has, I am told, raised its cost by
nearly two hundred per cent. I have seen some
fine specimens of Miaco ware, an opaque composition with a rough and unglazed surface; but
none of these Japanese manufactures that I
have met with equal the better specimens of old
porcelain, which I subsequently saw in the north
of China.

The bronzes exposed for sale at Yokuhama are
principally modern, but now and then an old and
valuable specimen may be found. At present
the value of these is becoming known; but when
the ports were first opened, I am assured that
merchants, in making purchases of copper for
shipment, not unfrequently found curious pieces
of old bronze surreptitiously introduced by the
Japanese traders as copper; and I myself, on my
first arrival, bought a very remarkable and ancient
specimen at its market value in copper by the

E

cattie.* The modern manufactures in bronze, though of very inferior metal, are often very handsome in form and workmanship; but these, also, have been doubled and trebled in price within a year or two.

In Yedo I have met with some very fine old bronzes of different descriptions of metal and in various forms. The most curious and rare is what they call the silver bronze, from there being an unusually large proportion of that metal in its composition. It has a wonderfully clear, musical ring, and I have never seen it but of the most polished and elaborate workmanship. Very old specimens — the inscriptions on some in my possession date back 800 years—are not un-common;† they consist principally in incense-burners, of various forms and sizes, generally re-presenting animals, such as bulls, deer, or cranes, and are composed of a very pure metal of a darker colour than European bronze.

* A cattie is about one-third more than the English pound avoirdupois—100 catties being equal to 133 lbs. These weights have been introduced into Japan from China.

† I should say, *were* not uncommon, for I hear that now they are extremely difficult to obtain.

Of bells I have seen some remarkably fine
specimens. As in China, they are sounded by
means of a blow from without, instead of by a
clapper; but I think the Chinese bell-metal
is superior to that of Japan.

The ivory carvings, which are worn by men
as buttons to sling their pipes upon, form an
important article of merchandise among the
curio-dealers; but there again the moderns fail
to keep pace with their forefathers—if not in
perfection of workmanship, certainly in original-
ity of design. These ivories are highly valued,
and always in exact proportion to their anti-
quity; and a Japanese points to the maker's
name upon his pipe-button with as much reverence as a collector with us would show in
the exhibition of the picture of a master, or the
rare edition of a favourite author. I have unfortunately forgotten the name of their Canova,
but had the good luck to obtain a very fine
specimen by him, though envious Britons tried
to make out that it was only a copy by one of
his favourite pupils. The subject is curious, and
points a useful moral. It represents a widow

unfaithful to the memory of her lord, who, in
revenge, is seen rising from his tomb behind her
back, and putting out his tongue at her; on one
side, a huge serpent, with distended jaws and
dart protruding, crawls towards her. On the
other side, a stern judge, with the Book of the
Law open before him, looks on approvingly.
There is hardly a phase of Japanese life or
character which may not be found represented
in these curious carvings. In minuteness of
detail and patient labour, the Chinese carvers of
ivory undoubtedly surpass the Japanese—but
the former are simply skilled mechanics, the
latter are artists—and their productions bear to
one another about the same relation that photo-
graphy bears to painting. Besides the articles
enumerated, which dazzle the eyes and damage
the pockets of the stranger visiting Japan, there
are many other curios to be acquired; and not
the least appreciated of my collection are the
charms, enamel beads, dolls, tops, and other toys,
all unique in their way; and you have only to
provide an intelligent shop-keeper with a pattern,
and he will reproduce, in Japanese materials,

your purse, your card-case or cigar-case, your pocket-book or your penknife ; and if you give him time, your revolver, your Chubb's lock, or your dressing-case.

If you give him kobangs,* there is not an article of your jewellery—ring, studs, watch-chain, or locket—which he will not manufacture at an almost nominal charge for workmanship. Given a pigskin, and he will even make you a hunting-saddle, which it requires some examination to distinguish from a veritable Peat.

Curio-hunting, however, was but the recreation of the few leisure hours which I could occasionally steal from my more serious and less agreeable occupations.

At first I thought, that having once obtained the consent of the Japanese Government to the exportation of horses, their acquisition would be simply an affair of time and money, for that

* A gold coin, of oval shape, intrinsically worth about 22 shillings ; when I arrived in Japan, these could be purchased for 6 itseboos, about 9 shillings ; when I left, Government was buying them up at the rate of 15 itseboos each.

horses existed in abundance was admitted, and
there was every disposition on the part of owners
to trade; but I soon found that in this, as in
every other transaction in Japan, the intervention of the authorities was indispensable. This
necessity entailed annoyances and delays against
which few tempers could remain proof.

Having been placed in direct communication
with the Governor and Vice-Governors of Kanagawa, these functionaries appointed officers of
various grades to attend to my wants; and as
each of these had his " ometske " or shadow to
act as a check upon him, I soon found myself
like the inspecting-generals in the newspapers,
—attended by a "numerous," if not a "brilliant
staff," — who — as " the staff " occasionally do
elsewhere—sadly. impeded the successful and
expeditious transaction of business.

All public business which the Governor of
Kanagawa, or his officers, have to do with, is
gone through at the Custom House, which contains also the local Treasury and the subordinate
branches of other departments of the State.
Here accordingly a number of two-sworded

officials are squatted on their mats, busy reading, writing, cyphering, and going through their various forms of business, from nine till four, without ever once being seen to read a newspaper, or to take any refreshment beyond occasional cups of tea.

They are very painstaking, methodical, and upon the whole very correct clerks. European merchants have their tempers sadly tried by them, for they will do their work in their own way, which is not an expeditious one ; but I had had some experience of public offices in England, and feel disposed to give the preference to my Japanese friends, as not a bit more obstructive, and a good deal more courteous, than their British colleagues.

Their system of account-keeping is, however, far more complicated even than that in force in our War Office, and in circumlocution they beat Pall Mall and Whitehall put together.

As an instance : I want to build stables, and having found a suitable site, apply to the Governor for leave to build on it; he must refer to Yedo. Authority obtained, after the usual delay, the Vice-Governors wish to consult with me on the matter. The officer charged with land matters is called upon for his opinion. The officer of public works is asked for his. The whole affair is referred back to the Governor— who refers back to Yedo, and in due time the site is placed at my disposal; but when I speak to my architect and builder—the prince of carpenters *—he shakes his head; he dare not work without the permission of the proper officers. Again I go to the Governor, and again the whole matter goes through the usual channels; and if, during the progress of the work, the slightest improvement suggests itself to me, I cannot have it carried out without further official reference.

When I commence to purchase horses, the

* These Japanese carpenters are wonderful workmen. I have had a good deal to do with them, and found them, one and all, very intelligent men, and more trustworthy than any of their class that I have met. They appeared to make it a point of honour to fulfil their agreements to the letter. Their trade, like most others in Japan, is hereditary; and my architect boasted of being the twenty-seventh of his family in direct descent. We have no such old firms as that, with all our boasting.

same provoking interference takes place; I am only allowed to buy from persons appointed by the Government, and in presence of the Yaconins; their patience and good-humour are inexhaustible — not so mine — and, day after day, they are by my side, noticing the colour, age, peculiarities, and price of every horse that passes into my possession, and at the conclusion of my day's labours adding up the total of the horses purchased, and of the money paid, with the most wonderful solicitude for the interests of the British public. Nor do their attentions cease here; for lest the dealers should be robbed of their itseboos or dollars, these kindhearted officials escort them on their way home, and generally manage to take care that none of the profits fall into improper hands.

In procuring the necessary supplies of horse equipment and forage, I was in like manner completely in the hands of the Yaconins, who levied a tax upon every item of my expenditure. It has been the fashion to describe Japanese officials as incorruptible; I am sorry to say that my experience does not justify such an opinion.

I do not know whether foreign representatives ever think it worth while to gain a public object, at the expense of a bribe;* but I do know that merchants, for their personal benefit, frequently obtain, by means of presents, what otherwise they might apply for in vain, and that they have long since discovered the secret of softening the rigour of trade regulations or consular laws.

Nearly the entire traffic of Japan is carried on by means of pack-horses; every gentleman or official of rank, moreover, prides himself upon having a large stable for the personal use of himself, his friends and retainers; and the right of breeding horses is not, as has been asserted, restricted to Daimios, but exists throughout the country among all classes; every seller, however, being liable to a tax on his profits.

From the practice of working them at an early age — two-year-olds frequently carrying heavy weights—perfect soundness is rarely met with among Japanese horses; and my dealers

* Our Foreign Office has a snug little fund available for such contingencies.

could not understand my objection to such
trifles as splints or spavins, or even a little down-
right lameness, which they would assure me did
not in the least interfere with the working
powers of their beasts. They certainly are good
weight-carriers for their size and make — six
piculs (about 800 lbs.) being an ordinary load
for a long journey; but they are possessed of
no one good point, being straggling, weedy brutes
(the average height is hardly above 13 hands),
with big heads, narrow chests, and drooping
hind quarters. They have all the national pre-
judice against foreigners, and display it more
openly than their masters. My entrance into
my stables was invariably the signal for an
universal commotion; but fear as a rule pre-
dominated over rage, though occasionally they
would lash out at me; and once a vicious brute
seized my hand between his teeth, and held it as
in a vice, until induced to relinquish it by the
application of a small crow-bar to his skull.
With their Japanese attendants they were, however, perfectly gentle and docile.

The Japanese do not feed their horses at

stated times, but let them eat whenever they are
not engaged in actual work. Their food consists
of chopped straw and water, or hay soaked in
water, and boiled peas, administered warm. I
tried to give them a taste for hard grain, but
they decidedly disapproved of all innovations
upon their established customs.

Farriery is an art much respected in Japan,
and the horse-doctor accordingly a person of
some repute. My English farrier occasionally
called in one of his native colleagues to consult
with in bad cases, and was surprised at the
intelligence and professional knowledge of these
men ;—they in their turn watched his mode of
treatment with the greatest attention and interest. Most of the diseases to which European
horses are subject prevail in Japan ;—but I lost
several of my horses from a disorder quite unknown with us,—which, commencing with the
symptoms of a violent cold or incipient glanders,
terminates fatally in a few hours. My farrier,
after a *post-mortem* examination in one of these
cases, found that the throat and stomach were
violently inflamed, and the blood throughout the

body in a state of corruption. It is noticeable that trifling wounds, such as hurts obtained by kicking in their stalls, or fighting with other horses, frequently induced locked-jaw.

The arts of shoeing and gelding horses are unknown in Japan, but my farrier gave instructions in both, and before leaving I not unfrequently saw the straw shoes in general use replaced by iron ones. Gelding is considered a barbarous and cruel practice, and is not likely to be introduced.

Japanese horse-dealers are quite as "sharp" in their practice as their *confrères* all the world over, and I must admit to having been, on more than one occasion, taken in by them. They judge by the same rule as we do, the marks of the teeth, of a horse's age. One of my dealers, —he deserves to be named—Onooma-Siodzi, resorted to the ingenious device of lacquering marks on the teeth of his animals, and nothing could exceed his hilarity and good-humour when I detected, and taxed him with, the fraud.

The Japanese is merciful to his beast. I never saw one of them ill-using his horses, nor have they ever the appearance of being starved or over-worked. Sore backs—that fruitful source of suffering in Europe—are almost unknown here. This I attribute to the form of saddle in use, * which, though very ugly and rather cumbersome to handle, perfectly protects the back and shoulders. All my horses were provided with these pack-saddles, but on their arrival

PACK-HORSES.

in China, a wise committee of British officers pronounced them " perfectly unsuited for the back of any known quadruped," and these saddles, with which Japanese horses carry their heavy loads from one end of the island to another, were condemned and allowed to rot as unserviceable, because two or three subaltern

* I refer to pack saddles; the riding saddle may, possibly, be comfortable for the horse, but is a terrible thing to bestride; the "led charger" of a Daimio, which, on State occasions, invariably forms a part of his procession, does not look happy: nothing is to be seen of him, so covered is he with trappings, but his legs, and these are generally puffed ; even his tail is tied up in a blue bag.

officers were too ignorant or too prejudiced to give them a trial.*

Extract from Diary, Jan. 24.—Captain Vyse held his first Consular Court to-day. The complainant, a British merchant of Yokuhama, charged one of his countrymen with shooting his dog. The dining-room was turned into a court of justice for the occasion, and the defendant, whom the Consul would insist upon addressing as prisoner, pleaded first, that he did not shoot the dog; secondly, that he had shot him in self-defence, and, thirdly, that the complainant never had a dog at all. There was a crowd of witnesses and hard swearing on both sides; indeed, all the Europeans of Yokuhama assembled " to see the fun." Fortunately, Vyse had not forgotten his orderly-room experiences, and so he maintained discipline and administered justice with military decision, common sense, and impartiality, if not with strict ac-

* On our visit to Fusi-jama, which occupied fourteen days, our baggage and stores were carried exclusively by pack-horses on these saddles, and though our packages were of various and unusual forms and sizes, the fourteen or sixteen horses performed their journey without a single break-down or derangement of their loads.

cordance to law. The "prisoner" being found
Guilty, was sentenced to pay a fine of one hundred and fifty dollars, such being the estimated
value of a good watch-dog in those unruly
times, and to apologize to the owner of the
murdered animal.

When the Gorogio, or Grand Council of State,
determined, by a considerable majority, to entertain Lord Elgin's demands for the conclusion
of a treaty of commerce, one of the principal
Daimios arose from his seat, and, half drawing
his sword from its scabbard, exclaimed,—" Let
traitors be false to the laws of their country and
the traditions of their ancestors; I, for one,
while I have life, will resist the admission of
the detested foreigner!" and so saying, he left
Yedo, accompanied by his retainers, and, se-
cluding himself in his remote dominions, became
and remains, one of the leaders of a large and
powerful party of anti-Europeans.

There cannot be a doubt that it went much
against the grain of even the most enlightened
of Japanese statesmen, to admit foreigners into
their country. Centuries of peace and national

prosperity had strengthened their convictions that their policy of perfect exclusiveness and isolation was the one most conducive to their welfare, and that there were no material wants which they could not supply within themselves, better than by any aid to be hoped for from so-called European civilization.

From the period of the last summary expulsion of Europeans down to the present times, Japan had not stood still; arts and sciences had flourished; institutions were consolidated and strengthened; laws had been relaxed in severity, and respect for them had increased in proportion; the powers of privileged classes had been restricted, but their lawful authority was more firmly established; the people had been relieved from burdens and disabilities, and their attachment to their rulers and their country had grown with their prosperity. What good would they derive from intercourse with foreigners? What could these teach them or bring them, that the mass of the people could want, or that the ruling powers would not dread? Well fed, well housed, well clothed, and enjoying a degree of material liberty beyond which they had no hopes or wishes, happy in their domestic relations, contented with their mode of life, and warmly attached to habits and customs hallowed by the tradition of ages—why should foreign traders be invited to come among them from remote lands, to arouse their discontent, or their avarice, to teach them artificial wants, or infect them with unknown vices?

Such were the arguments of Japanese conservatives and protectionists, and what had we to say in reply? International relations, we told them, are a necessary condition to political progress; but their institutions had stood the test of ages without such aid, and they had not retrograded. Commercial intercourse would advance them in civilization; but they were not barbarians: and would the example of trading adventurers tend to improve a simple-minded, courteous, and gentle-mannered people? Christianity would smooth their paths on earth and open for them a way to heaven; but they remembered of old, how missionaries, professing a religion of submission and peace, preached doctrines of rebellion, and caused bloodshed throughout the land; and their own gods knew the way to heaven as well as ours. No, they did not want us; they were quite satisfied to remain as they were, and what right had foreigners to intrude upon their privacy?

Some of their objections were unanswerable; but Lord Elgin came with the *prestige* of a recent diplomatic victory (as was fancied) over the stubborn Court of Pekin, and he had, more-over, those Boom-Boom Funis * at his back; and then there are liberal and free-trade states-men even in Japan, who were ready to be con-vinced that they might easily double and treble their revenues by a little judicious commerce; and then we only asked them to admit a few Englishmen, under the strict surveillance of consuls, into their outlying ports; and then an alliance with a great European Power would be so useful to them in case of accidents; and then (what a row those guns from our ships make as

* Funi is the Japanese for ship, and men-of-war are dis-tinguished from other vessels by the " Boom-Boom " of their guns.

they salute!) the Queen had sent a high officer all the way from England, and Her Majesty would indeed feel surprised and hurt if her royal and well-beloved cousin, the Tycoon, &c., &c., &c.; and so we got our treaty, and the small end of the wedge was inserted, and who can tell what will follow?

Can we be surprised that this sweeping reform—or, more correctly speaking, this revolution—should be unpopular among a large portion of the ruling classes in Japan? It is useless to attempt to gloss over our motives, as some trading missionaries do, with philanthropic or religious pretences. It is not true that we resort to Japan to civilize, for civilization exists already; or to convert the heathen, for such attempts are strictly prohibited under the terms of the treaty which we have accepted; or to add to the happiness of the people, for a more contented people does not live; or for any object in the world but to trade with profit to ourselves. And this must be patent to the Japanese themselves, who may probably become rich by intercourse with our merchants, but who are hardly likely to be in other respects improved by it.

The so-called pioneers of civilization are, like other pioneers, more noted for physical energy than for gentler or more refined qualities. It is not the skilled or scientific farmer, but the strong-armed labourer, who cuts down the forest; nor is it the liberal, enlightened, prudent, and educated merchant, but the daring, money-seeking adventurer, who clears the way for commerce. What have the Japanese to learn from such men? Do they set them a profitable example in morality, in decency, in religion, in probity, in intelligence, in industry, or even in the outward forms of social intercourse? *

We decry the Japanese as a depraved and profligate race, devoid of shame and modesty; but does not the European who takes up his abode among them very readily adopt their ways, and frequently surpass them in their

* Let me guard myself against the suspicion of either personality or sweeping condemnation. I believe there are not a few among the European merchants in Japan, who would fully concur in my remarks, which, of course, apply only to a class; but that class is, unfortunately, a large one.

vices? We call their religion a gross superstition; but do our traders always profess any religion whatever? We say the Japanese are false; but did we teach them truthfulness or honesty when we bought their gold weight for weight with silver, and drained their treasury of native currency by false representations? We call them a semi-barbarous race; but contrast the courteous, dignified bearing, and the invariable equanimity of temper of the lowest official or smallest tradesman, with the insolent arrogance and swagger, the still more insolent familiarity, or the besotted violence, of many an European resident or visitor!

Let our traders indulge in no boasts of superiority or professions of disinterestedness, but be content to establish friendly commercial relations with the Japanese; to introduce all that they will accept of ours; to receive all that we require of theirs; and, while gradually developing the incalculable resources of a new and splendid country, reap a golden harvest from their energy and enterprise.

If our Government can help them to do this

without dishonour, without injustice, without outraging the feelings, or, if you will, the prejudices of a friendly people, then may our commerce prosper! But sooner than enrich our traders at the price of Japanese blood or of English good faith—sooner than carry war into that fair land, and rapine, fire, and murder among those happy, smiling homesteads—let us tear our treaty into shreds, and withdraw our flag for ever from the shores and waters of Japan!

Hitherto, our merchants have had no reason to complain of their success. In spite of many unnecessary restrictions, and continual official interference and obstruction, the profits have, as they themselves state, " exceeded their most sanguine expectations." Let them be moderate, and not risk killing their gold-egg-laying goose. Upon their conduct, upon their wisdom, upon their good sense, and not upon diplomatic treaties or consular regulations, depends, as far as Europeans are concerned, the future of Japan. In the natural course of things it will be discovered by the Japanese that commerce, like mercy, " blesses him that gives and him that takes ;" and in proportion as this becomes felt, European intercourse will extend, and friendly feeling between natives and foreigners increase. Fanaticism may occasionally lead to acts of crime and violence; assassins may be again, as they have been before, the agents of individual vengeance or political intrigue; but let them be assured that nothing but their own folly, recklessness, or bad faith, can by possibility lead to another general expulsion or massacre of Europeans in Japan.

The Japanese, like the Chinese, New Year is celebrated towards the end of January; and this is, accordingly, a season of universal idleness, debauchery, and devotion. The streets are filled with arches of bamboo and evergreens. The houses are decorated with multi-coloured banners of paper and cotton; the people of all ranks are clad in their gayest holiday attire; shops are closed, and priests and tea-house keepers reap a rich harvest. Looking from my bedroom window into the temple grounds upon which the

Consulate stands, I see numerous groups wandering among the graves, some praying earnestly, others pouring water into the trough at the foot of the tombstone to refresh the dead beneath; others, again, planting shrubs and flowers, or reverently, and with a simple faith, more touching and, I doubt not, more sincere than the most ostentatious display of piety, laying their offerings upon the last resting-places of those dear to them. I saw a rosy-cheeked child stand on tiptoe to hang a fresh wreath upon a tombstone; then it poured a tiny cup of water into the trough, and having thus attended to the creature comforts of a departed parent, brother, or sister, the little thing kissed the stone and toddled off. Would there were no worse superstitions in the world than this!

As well as I could judge, religion, or, at any rate, its outward observance, is left pretty much to women and children, under the guidance and instruction of the bonza, or priest, who may generally be known by a sleek, well-fed appearance, and a shaven skull. Men seem to be above the weakness of propitiating their deities by prayer or fees, and find in tea-houses metal more attractive than in the temples.

The Japanese, like their Celestial brethren across the way, are certainly a very pleasure-loving people, and the Government, as paternal governments are apt to do all the world over, from Vienna to Yedo, foster this feeling, and encourage all public amusements as the surest antidote to political aspirations. Were the re-creation of the Japanese peasant, mechanic, or tradesman limited to compulsory absence from labour on fifty-two days in the year, during which every place of entertainment or interest should be closed against him, and all around rendered as gloomy and sombre as possible, he would probably become morose, discontented, and dangerous; he would brood over his lot, grumble and reason, start a debating society and a club, and end either by being sawed in two as a rebel, or elected the President of an Eastern Republic.

But frequent festivals, the cheap amusements of which are promoted, and to a certain extent joined in, by the officials, leave him no time to reflect upon his wrongs, or if they do, his comrades are too busy enjoying themselves to attend to his grievances. There may be a great deal of work, very small pay, and the chances of a prison or a beating to-morrow; but to-day, the tea-house, with its music and its moosmes, its saki and its masks, the fair, the theatre, the wrestlers, and the dance. A few tempos* pay for all. So, *Vive le jeu! Vive le Daimio! Vive le Japon!*

I am told that in Yedo and other large cities desperate fights between the followers of different Daimios take place on occasion of these gatherings; but, though I saw a great many drunken swashbucklers, with flushed faces and a more than ordinary swagger, in the crowds of Kanagawa and Yokuhama, no disturbance took place during the new year's festivities, nor were any of the foreigners, who mixed freely with the populace, molested or insulted. It is probable, however, that extraordinary precautions had been taken in these places to preserve the peace.

I remember at the time hearing this entire absence of ill-feeling on the part of the Japanese

* An oval copper coin, of the value of one penny.

towards Europeans cited as a proof that the stories we heard of their repugnance towards us, and of their bloodthirstiness, were mere fables; but a day or two only elapsed before we learnt that murder—deliberate, long-planned murder —might be committed in the full light of day, and, provided the victim were publicly obnoxious, with as much impunity as would attend a legalized execution.

The following extract from one of my private letters, dated in the beginning of February, 1860, tells the story :—

" On the night of the 30th, I was aroused from sleep by a messenger from Yedo, who announced the assassination, in broad daylight, and at the gate of the Legation, of Dan, Mr. Alcock's steward, by birth a Japanese, who having been wrecked on the coast of China, had been carried to America, where he remained seven years, and acquired a perfect knowledge of English; he was therefore invaluable to Mr. Alcock as *homme d'affaires* and *maître d'hôtel.* The poor fellow had long been aware that his life was in danger, for not only were the authorities extremely jealous of his knowledge of Japanese affairs, which rendered him a dangerous *employé* at a foreign Legation, but he was very proud of his position as a confidential servant to the British Minister, and gave himself great airs among his countrymen on the strength of it, wore the European costume, treated the Yaconins who formed the Embassy guard with hauteur, and went so far as to interfere, in the interests of his master, with their privilege of levying black mail on Mr. Alcock's tradespeople. Hico, likewise an Americanized Japanese, now a thriving merchant under the stars and stripes at Yokuhama, and who had known Dan in the United States, warned him repeatedly of his danger, and urged him to adopt a more conciliatory manner ; but Dan was deaf to his friend's advice, and relying upon the protection of Mr. Alcock's flag and Colonel Colt's revolver (which latter he carried conspicuously at his waist), continued to swagger and to defy his countrymen. This was not his only offence ; there were rumours of ' an affair in which a lady was concerned ' (an American education had not improved Dan's morals), so that he had both love and hate to answer for. So notorious was his danger, that the Governor of Yedo waited on Mr. Alcock a few days since, and requested him to send Dan out of the country as a person obnoxious to the authorities ; but as no greater crime than being disliked could be alleged against him, Mr. Alcock, of course, declined to accede to the request.

"On the 30th, Dan, having returned from escorting Mr. Alcock on his daily ride, was leaning against the flagstaff of the Legation, and talking to some little children from an adjoining house, when a short sword was thrust through his body from behind and left there, the murderer disappearing down an alley. The poor fellow staggered a few paces, and at that moment Mr. Eusden, the Vice-consul, rode up and asked him what was the matter. 'Draw out the sword,' was the faint reply ; and as the weapon was withdrawn, poor Dan uttered a groan and dropped dead.

" This murder has created no little consternation here. Who, they say, is safe, when an *employé* of the Legation can be cut down in open day, and literally under the shadow of the British flag?

"The Ministers were full of expressions of regret, and promised to use every effort to trace the culprit, and all the authorities are profuse in condolence and offers of assistance. Mr. Alcock placed little faith in their professions: he requested, however, that in order to mark in a public manner their detestation of the deed, the principal functionaries of Yedo should attend the funeral of the murdered man. They assented; but when, at the appointed hour, the procession was about to start, they sent their excuses, pleading that it would be quite contrary to custom for Japanese officials to be present on such an occasion. And now the British Lion was aroused with a vengeance, nor did he show his teeth and shake his mane in vain,* for within an hour after the excuses had been received, two pale-faced governors, in full dress, with a host of Yaconins of various ranks, might have been seen demurely walking in the *cortège,* to the

* The opportune presence of H.M.S. *Cruiser* may have contributed to bring the authorities to their senses.

astonishment and dismay of the assembled thousands who lined the streets of Yedo; nor did they dare to return homewards until the earth had fallen upon the coffin of poor Dan."

One of the many difficulties with which I had to contend, in the management of my stables, was getting the horses exercised. None but a two-sworded man is allowed to ride in Japan, and my bettos, or grooms, disapproved of leading horses for a walk, and when compelled to do so, were no sooner out of my sight than they tied their beasts up at a tea-house door, and passed their afternoons in the quiet and undisturbed enjoyment of their *dolce far niente.*

Occasionally, I attempted to remedy this, by placing myself at the head of my " Irregular Horse," and leading them out into the country, where there were no Yaconins to notice my innocent infraction of the law. It was curious to behold three or four hundred wild ponies, mounted, barebacked, by bettos wearing no other clothing than a narrow strip of cotton around their loins, scampering along the narrow paths of paddy-fields, or up the steep mountain roads, utterly reckless of danger, and greeting the occasional mishaps of their fellows with shouts of hilarious laughter.

On one of these occasions, a thin-skinned trooper, who had fallen out of the ranks during the march, was met on his way home to stables by a party of unruly Britons from Yokuhama, who took possession of his horse, which was subsequently traced to the possession of a gentleman of the Hebrew persuasion. This youth could not, in the face of a clearly-branded V.R., dispute the identity of the animal, and expiated his "lark" (for nothing more serious was intended) in a Consular Court.*

I was indignantly protesting against this violation of the sanctity of the Queen's stud,

---

* This was the same young Israelite who, at a later period, was sentenced to deportation from Japan for shooting a Yaconin. The act was not intentional, but committed in a paroxysm of fear; but an example was much wanted at the time, and this silly, but by no means dangerous young man, became the victim. The sentence was hardly necessary, however; a braver man than our Jew would have deported himself after killing a Japanese official.

when a Yaconin was announced, who informed
the interpreter that an "accident" had happened to some Europeans at Yokuhama. This
accident, it appears, was nothing less than the
murder of two Dutch ship-captains, who had
been cut down in the streets by unknown assassins. We immediately started for the scene.
On our way across the Bay, the Governor's
barge, with its monstrous lanterns, passed us
rapidly; he was going to face the storm of
European indignation. In the streets of Yokuhama we met a strong picquet of Russian
marines, who had been landed—armed to the
teeth — from His Imperial Majesty's ship *Ja-*
ponitch, and on entering the "hotel" (where the
bodies lay) we were challenged by the hoarse
voice of a gigantic sentry, before being admitted
into the *salle-à-manger,* which had been converted into a guard-room, and where hairy Mus-
covites smoked in sullen silence. These fellows
looked very dirty and savage, and vividly recalled
to my recollection old Crimean days, when the
same flat faces under the same flat caps used to
scowl at us.

I have witnessed some ugly scenes in the course of my life, but a more ghastly sight than the mutilated bodies of these poor murdered Dutchmen I never beheld. Truly, those Japanese blades do not do their work by halves, and a second blow is seldom necessary. One of the victims was a grey-haired man ; he had been, as usual, struck from behind, and his face was almost cut in two. The other was of middle age ; his hand had been severed at the wrist, and was found nearly fifty yards from the body. It is supposed that it had been cut off on his attempting to draw his revolver; that he then ran, and was pursued, and cut down by a blow which laid his shoulder open to the lungs.

A number of Dutchmen stood around the bodies, with pale faces, and strong oaths on their lips. They have many an old grudge against the Japanese ; they remember how, but a few years since, they had to prostrate themselves before a Yaconin, and to eat endless dirt with their silk and their kobangs; and now that they see resolute Englishmen and Americans, and armed Russians by their side, they long for

vengeance; but swearing will do no good. One
sensible Hollander, who has been crying bitterly
over his countrymen, hopes that his Consul will
insist upon the Japanese· paying a pension to
the families of the murdered, which he ventures
to think would be "more goot dan hang de tief."

I accompanied Captain Vyse into the Audience
Hall, where the Governor sat, surrounded by his
officers. He smiled blandly, and seemed somewhat at a loss when our Consul, in a tone more
decided than diplomatic, inquired into the cause
of his mirth, and hinted that the murder of
Europeans was no laughing matter, as he might
find out some day to his cost; and then followed an interminable discussion, ending, as
usual, in nothing. It was evident that at least
two men had been engaged in the foul act, but,
though committed in the main street, and while
shops were still open and people walking about,
no one had seen or heard anything. Of course,
every effort should be made to trace the
assassins ; but of course, these, as do all other
murderers of Europeans in Japan, remain undis-
covered.

It was not alleged that any provocation could have been given by the two Dutchmen; their countrymen knew them to be remarkably quiet, inoffensive men, and they had been cut down on their way to their boats, after leaving a shop in the main street, where they had bought some baubles and toys, probably for the wives and children who were praying, in some quaint, clean town far away in Holland, for the husbands and fathers whom they should see no more on earth.

As Captain Vyse's interview drew towards a conclusion, the American Consul entered with a fresh stock of indignation, which he poured forth volubly upon the unfortunate Governor, who bore it with the usual exemplary patience and good temper of Japanese officials. After all, what could he do? The men were dead, and the murderers would be punished, when caught; and so a patrol of the town to see that the necessary steps had been taken to apprehend the culprit, was proposed. The Governor assented very unwillingly to this arrangement; for it is not usual for so high an official to stroll about the streets after midnight, with irate

Consuls at his side, and a Russian picquet behind him; but there was no resisting on such an occasion, and we traversed the town, and inspected the police arrangements, than which nothing could be more admirably calculated to facilitate escape. All the stations and guard-houses were brilliantly illuminated; here and there strings of lanterns were extended across the principal streets; and as if this was not enough to warn the assassins to keep out of the way, small parties of police perambulated the town, always giving due notice of their approach by loudly rattling their iron rings, and otherwise proclaiming their presence.

Having reached the landing-place, the Governor hoped that the Consuls were satisfied with his exertions, and, bowing courteously, entered his barge and departed.

We also turned homewards, but, *en route*, the American Consul announced, in a solemn manner, that a duty yet remained to be done. I was sleepy, and urged that it might be deferred until the morning, or, rather, the day—for it was long past midnight.

" No, *sir*," he replied, with that peculiar sent
tentious manner in which an American frames
and glazes his most commonplace remarks.
" *Ex*cuse me, but it must be performed *to*-night,'
and you, sir, will *not, I* trust, refuse *to* lend us
your *as*sistance." .Impressed with the importance of the occasion, we accompanied him to his
Consulate, where it turned out that the discussion of pâtés and champagne cocktails formed
the important business that could not be deferred, and it was not without difficulty that we
were able to excuse ourselves from his invitation to stay to breakfast, and to make our escape
from our ever-hospitable friend.

Extracts from my Diary, Feb. 27.—Rode to
Yedo with Captain Colvile, H.M.S. *Camilla.*
Mr. Alcock had an interview to-day with the
authorities, on the subject of the murder of the
Dutchmen. The Government appear alarmed,
and profess great anxiety. They are fortifying
the Legations, increasing the guards, and urge
that Europeans shall not appear in Yedo without a Japanese escort. This places the foreign representatives in a dilemma; if they consent to native guards and escorts, they will virtually be prisoners in their residences—surrounded by spies night and day—and subject to extra taxation upon all necessaries of life that enter their gates. If, on the other hand, they refuse, the Government may disclaim all further responsibility as to their safety, and throw all consequences upon the foreigners' rashness.

On our way to Yedo we had, by order of the Governor of Kanagawa, been escorted by two mounted Yaconins; and though we rode part of the way across country and at a rattling pace, our guards — albeit unused to the sporting mood — followed close at our heels, scrambled through whatever obstacles they could not get over, and, in spite of several "croppers," entered Yedo in our company, highly delighted with their exploit.

Feb. 28.—Heavy fall of snow; thermometer 24°. Went out with Colvile and several Yaconins, curio-hunting in the main streets of Yedo, but no success; the shopkeepers, for some unexplained reason or other, declined to sell their wares to us, and the crowds that followed, and surrounded us when we stopped, made our expedition unpleasant. Returned to breakfast, where met M. de Bellecourt, French Consul-General, who informed me that, upon the whole, he was really disposed to prefer Paris to Yedo; Mr. Townshend Harris, the United States Minister; and Mr. Euskin, his secretary and interpreter, who probably knows more of Japan and the Japanese, and speaks their language more fluently than any living European.*

The lives necessarily led by the members of the Foreign Legations in Yedo are not enviable. In Kanagawa and Yokuhama, Europeans are free to come and go when and where they will, within

* Poor Euskin was assassinated a few months afterwards, while in the act of mounting his horse at the residence of the Prussian Ambassador, whom he had prominently assisted in concluding a somewhat unpopular treaty. This had, no doubt, rendered him obnoxious to the Conservative party. In private life, he was an universal favourite among all classes, and well he might be so, for a more gentle, kind-hearted man never lived. Although a Dutchman by birth, and occupying a subordinate diplomatic position, America is mainly indebted to him for its influence in Japan.

defined limits; they have ceased to be extraordinary novelties, or objects of wonder or dislike; but in the capital, the *Tojin* is either a public show, and viewed much as a newly-imported reptile in a menagerie, or a prisoner within his walls. The American, French, and English Legations are at considerable distances from each other, which it is unsafe to traverse without an escort. Intercourse between them is, therefore, less frequent than might be expected; walking is out of the question, on account of the mobs; shooting is prohibited; and beyond the afternoon riding party—again with an escort —there is no out-door amusement. To make matters worse, communication with the rest of the world is rare and uncertain; occasionally, a vessel of war appears, but she cannot approach within five or six miles of the shore. When a mäil comes in, and English letters from three to six months old have been devoured, it becomes hard work to read up the *Times*, from the earliest dates; and ignorance of local topics or current gossip deadens *Punch's* best jokes. Writing despatches, and fighting Japanese officials, through the medium of two interpreters, may be very entertaining, but even that becomes wearisome.

Mr. Alcock is a man of refined and literary tastes, and his *employés* are all, more or less, disposed to occupy themselves in the study of the language and institutions of Japan; but still, when I saw them spelling over an old copy of Kaempfner, or an unintelligible Japanese grammar, or feeding the gold fish in the pond, or looking westward at space through a telescope, I could not but congratulate myself that I was not a servant of the Foreign Office, doomed to pass the best part of a precarious life in Yedo.

The Governors called upon Mr. Alcock to-day, and at the conclusion of their interview he presented one of them with a coloured lithograph of the *Great Eastern* steam-ship, duly mounted on silk and rollers, and was proceeding to explain matters, when the Governor assured him that he knew all about the big ship; that she was a dead failure,* and that it was strange that a great naval Power like

* This was in February, 1860.

ours should have committed so many blunders as attended the building of this monster steamer.

It is wonderful how well versed the better classes of Japanese are in European affairs, and with what eagerness they seek for information, taking good care, by inviting opinions from different quarters, to guard themselves against being misled through pardonable national predilections. Thus, a few homely truths from Mr. Alcock would be required to reduce the greatness and power of the United States to possible dimensions; Mr. Harris's version of the American War of Independence would be taken into due account in the consideration of our military capacities; and, if the French representative laughed at the pretensions of a non-naval Power like Prussia claiming a treaty with Japan, our inquisitive friends had heard how a certain Prussian general named Blücher had taken a prominent part in shutting up Napoleon Bonaparte in St. Helena. Russia, I think, enjoys the greatest *prestige* in Japan, as a political, military, and naval Power, and the one most to be feared, if not respected; and this opinion she loses no opportunity of strengthening.*

Feb. 29.—M. de Bellecourt had arranged that he would accompany me to Kanagawa to-day in order to attend the funeral of the murdered Dutchmen, and had warned his Yaconins to be in readiness to escort him after breakfast. At the appointed time, however, a message came to inform us that the river was too much swollen to admit of our crossing, and that we should have to postpone our departure. Unfortunately for our friends, this statement was invalidated by the opportune arrival of the Kanagawa letter-carrier, who had found no difficulty in crossing the ferry. This pretext having failed, it was alleged that the Yaconins had used up all their horses, and that a day's rest for these poor animals was indispensable. M. de Bellecourt with politeness and humanity placed his stable at the

---

* For one English, one meets three or four Russian ships of war in Japanese waters, and their naval diplomatists prove irresistible.

disposal of the officers ; then followed half-a-dozen
other objections, more and more puerile, till, on
the Consul-General saying that he *would* go, with
or without Yaconins, the truth came out.   There
was, it appears, a large procession on its way
to Yedo, comprising no less a person than the
daughter of the Mikado coming to be wedded to
a great prince. She was attended by all her ladies
and gentlemen, and an enormous *suite* of armed
followers.   It would never do for us to meet
them on the road.   M. de Bellecourt, however,
saw no objection ; he would be *desolé* to miss
such an opportunity of showing his respect for a
Japanese princess, and only too *charmé* to see
her armed retainers, for whom he felt the greatest
regard *d'avance*.   But the thing was impossible.
Mais non—on the contrary ; and so we started,
and had gone only a few hundred yards when our
Yaconins came galloping at our heels, and took
up their position—one as *avant courier*, the other
two in our rear : our bettos, as usual, running
beside our horses.

We had proceeded about five miles on our
way, when the advanced guard of the procession

came in sight. This was principally composed of inferior officers in charge of baggage, contained in large black lacquer cases, like exaggerated despatch-boxes, carried on poles. Verily the *trousseau* of a Japanese princess is a splendid affair, since the nuptial *impedimenta* formed an unbroken column of nearly four miles.

By the time we arrived at the river, the *cortège* assumed a more distinguished appearance; the norrimons were larger, their poles more curved, and various emblems, indicative of rank, were borne before them. Our Yaconins now showed symptoms of nervousness, and the Consular bettos slunk a trifle to the rear.

We crossed the river, which was not swollen, as the Yaconins laughingly admitted; but they urged us to go no further, but to await the passage of the procession in a tea-house, where, hidden from view, we might observe it. So imploringly did they plead, so significantly did they draw their hands across their throats in token of the fate that awaited them if we persevered, that I should have been disposed to give way. M. de Bellecourt, however, said that a lesson inculcating

the sanctity attaching to the person of the representative of the Emperor of the French was
indispensably necessary, and that there could
not be a better opportunity of asserting the
right of an European to proceed, without let or
hindrance, along the high road, no matter who
might pass. We accordingly rode on, single
file, and on the side of the road, so as to avoid
possibly interfering with the order of the procession. The Yaconins were now fairly at their wits'
end; at first they dismounted and led their
horses; then, as some savage-looking members
of the procession shouted at them, they made a
last desperate attempt to turn us back, and
finding us inexorable, they fairly turned tail
and vanished, man and horse, leaving us to our
fate; nor did we see them again, until they
overtook us near Kanagawa, in high good-humour, and with a full determination to protect
us against any possible danger. M. de Bellecourt's two grooms, with monstrous deformed
eagles emblazoned on their coats, could not resist the example of their superiors, and disappeared suddenly, but my betto proved faithful,

and walked by my side, perfectly heedless of the scowls and imprecations of his countrymen.*

As we progressed, we were repeatedly motioned to stop or turn back, and at length a two-sworded man approached, and laid his hand upon my bridle. A gentle tap over his knuckles from my whip induced him to relinquish his hold, but our position was becoming unpleasant. As far as we could look before us, on the straight road, we saw nothing but armed men, to every one of whom our presence was an affront ; but retreat was as dangerous as advance, and to have got off our horses and stood in the road would, it appears, have been derogatory to our characters as European gentlemen. Several officials now placed themselves in our path, as if to check our progress. M. Bellecourt, in the most polite manner, assured them, in purest Parisian accent, that " *Comme Chargé d'Affaires de l'Empereur Napoleon il s'arrêterait pas, soit même pour Sa Majesté le Mikado,*"

---

* A few days later, an official at Kanagawa asked me the name of the betto who had accompanied me from Yedo, but divining the object of the inquiry, I declined to gratify his curiosity.

while I wished myself in a stable full of my
most vicious horses, in preference to my present
position.   Again we proceeded—again were we
stopped ; and this time, a consultation was held
around the norrimon of a man of high rank,
at the end of which a gentleman dressed
marvellously like the Knave of Clubs, and
bearing the largest fan I ever saw, even at a
pantomime, rushed up, and, walking by our side,
made way for us, and enabled us to pass the
whole *cortège* without further molestation.

And now *the* norrimon approaches.   The principal men preceding it are mounted, and around
them are foot-soldiers, carrying matchlocks and
crossbows.   The Knave of Clubs prostrates himself before the chair ; we pull up and salute the
invisible princess ; then come more cavaliers,
and more armed men ; by degrees, the norrimons
become smaller, as their occupants dwindle down
from relatives of the bride and maids of honour,
to servants ; then comes more baggage, a few
stragglers bringing up the rear, and the Knave
of Clubs, having played his game out, makes a
parting bow.   We say "Allegato," and "Sio-

nada," at which he laughs ; and, with a wave of the big fan, he shuffles off, and turns up no more.

We bragged a good deal at Vyse's dinner-table in the evening about having so pluckily maintained the dignity of our respective countries, but I suspect we both wished ourselves well out of it at the time. Vyse thinks that the old B troop would have made short work of the whole procession, which I take the liberty of doubting.

Almost every European, including the officers and crews of the ships in harbour, attended the funeral of the poor Dutchmen ; the Governor, however, made his excuses, whereupon Captain Schott, commander of the *Japonitch*, entered the Custom-house at the head of his marines, and informed his Japanese Excellency that he had the greatest possible respect for him and no intention whatever of dictating, but that he must insist upon his immediately falling in, as the funeral could not possibly take place without him. The Governor turns helplessly to the

English Consul, and inquires what would be the consequences of his refusal. That functionary shakes his head solemnly, ominously, as if the alternative were too horrible to mention; but Captain Schott declares that if the Russian flag were insulted (what the Russian flag has to do in the matter does not clearly appear) his guns should open fire upon the town.

A few minutes later, the funeral procession moved off; and, for the third time* in about six months, a Japanese Governor, with his suite, were seen to assist in paying the last honours over the graves of murdered Europeans.

There was great consternation in Yokuhama for some time after the murder of the Dutchmen, and revolvers rose one hundred per cent. in value. Those who associate the agents of com-

----

* The first victim was an officer of the Russian navy, who, having landed at Yokuhama with four sailors to purchase provisions, was cut down on returning to his boats. Although a Russian squadron under Admiral Count Poutatien was lying in the harbour, and extraordinary pressure was put upon the Government, the assassin was not discovered.

merce with peace and smugness, with a decent suit of black, and a portly, respectable presence, would be amazed to see our merchants as, in slouched hats and fancy dresses, bearded like pards, and bristling with fire-arms, they savagely buy their silk and sell their cotton, or, with fierce gestures, superintend the shipment of their goods, determined to defraud the Custom-house or perish in the attempt.

An endeavour was made by them to organize a Committee of Safety in the shape of an European Police Force; but the Yokuhama Volunteers, though willing enough to command or direct, objected strongly to obey or to work. National rivalries arose between English and Americans; the one solitary representative of French commerce in Japan broke out into open mutiny because he was not invested with a high command; and the Dutchmen seceded in a body because night duty was imposed upon them.

Meanwhile, rumours of an universal massacre became prevalent, and the Japanese doubled their barriers and guards, and closely watched all who entered the settlement.

About this time, I happened to dine with Captain Vyse and M. de Bellecourt on board the *Camilla*, and Captain Colvile fired a salute in honour of the latter gentleman as we left his ship.* The commander of the Russian brig *Japonitch*, for some reason or other, chose to imagine that these guns were fired in his honour, and immediately replied with a corresponding volley. M. de Bellecourt took the Russian salute as a compliment to himself, and insisted upon going on board to acknowledge it. Captain Schott received us most kindly, produced—as every Russian sailor seems to think himself bound to do—champagne and porter (he drank them alternately), and when at length we succeeded in effecting our escape from his hospitable custody, he fired a salute to each of the Consuls.

These unusual sounds had roused all Kanagawa and Yokuhama; the Governor, startled

---

* No formal salute can, I believe, be fired after sunset from a man-of-war; but, being anxious to do honour to his French guest, Captain Colvile compromised matters by going through the periodical practice of "beating to quarters," which answered the same purpose as a salute.

from his sleep, ordered out his barge and prepared
to seek his post. The Treasury and Custom-
house were illuminated; lanterns moved rapidly
and in all directions along the shores; Yaconins
emerged from their dwellings in blank amazement; and Europeans hastily huddled on their
clothes, and looked to the caps of their revolvers.

The night was calm, and, borne upon a
southern breeze, the boom of cannon reached
the capital, where panic-stricken functionaries
met to lament the bombardment of Kanagawa,
and the British Minister and his *attachés*, in the
lightest of clothing, held a shivering consultation, and wondered whether there were any
survivors to tell the tale of the European
massacre, which it was evident the ships of war
were revenging.

The last gun from the *Japonitch* had hardly
been fired, when a Russian boat passed us. She
was full of armed sailors, and the officer in
charge on recognizing us called out in French
that a Consul had just been murdered in Yokuhama; so we turned our head in that direction

and landed. It was not a Consul, we were informed by a pale Dutchman, only an interpreter; he was not dead, we heard next, only wounded; the Yaconins knew nothing. The Governor sat smiling blandly at his post: he had heard no report whatever except that of the guns, which he was quite at a loss to account for. Messengers were sent in all directions to make inquiries, and soon the unconscious victim of supposed assassination was found in the shape of a British sailor, lying dead drunk in the street, with an empty bottle clasped affectionately in his arms.

* * * * *

Mr. Alcock gives a *déjeûner* at Ojee, the great tea-garden near Yedo, whither, at this season, all classes, from the princely Daimio to the small trader, resort, *en famille*, for a day's fresh air and recreation. It is a lovely spring morning; the hedges are bright with early buds and flowers, and the sun seems to coquette with the young leaves and the sweet-smelling herbs, as now he smiles in his full brightness, now hides his face behind a cloud, and sheds a gentle shower of happy tears—whereupon we drop metaphor, and put on our waterproofs. Mr. Harris, beside whom I am riding, must be responsible for my poetical mood, for he is enthusiastic in his admiration of his beloved Japan, and expatiates upon her beauties with all the ardour of an elderly lover contemplating the charms of a youthful *fiancée.* Love, it is true, is blind, and my companion is too enraptured to be sensible to any blemishes in the object of his devotion. In his eyes, she is perfection ; her faults of temper are high spirit— her waywardness is character—her extravagance is generosity—nay, even her somewhat loose morals are only the outbreaks of a playful dis- position. Those who criticise his mistress are ill-natured, jealous, intolerant. Why should I try to disturb his faith in her? So I ride along, and own that she certainly is very beautiful, that her manners are charming, and though her education has been somewhat neglected, that she does not want for brains—*au reste, I* am not going to marry her, so it is none of my busi- ness.

The ride to Ojee is through a lovely and love-

able country, and some of the views from the
heights are marvels of landscape. Leaving our
horses at the tea-house, while hampers are un-
packed and breakfast prepared—for we are not
yet sufficiently acclimatized to affect Japanese
chow-chow—we walked, through lanes hedged by
bushes of tea (which, for the first time, I discovered to be of the camelia tribe) and a magnificent park, in which Nature had most bountifully
provided for the payment of gentlemen's debts,
to Inari—the Temple of the Foxes—the presiding
deity of which is celebrated for his success in the
cure of barrenness. None of our party required
the services of this particular god, so we contented ourselves with buying, for a few pence,
a stamped paper which was warranted to prove
a certain charm against a violent death — no
unwise precaution in these times.

On our way home we passed Gongen Sama,
known as the Tycoon's Hunting-Lodge; but it
must indeed be a long bow that would reach this
from his palace-windows in Yedo: or is it possible
that, after all, His Majesty is not kept so close
a prisoner, and that he occasionally gets about

" *niebon*" ? * Our attendants would or could not enlighten us on this point.

The Government really appears in earnest in wishing to afford all possible protection to Europeans. We had been escorted by at least a dozen Yaconins during our ride, and, on arriving at Ojee, found no less than forty more awaiting us. They informed Mr. Alcock that they had been sent to attend him and his party, and nothing could exceed their watchful anxiety for our safety.

The grounds about Ojee are prettily laid out, and ornamented with fish-ponds, fountains, and grottoes; but the practice introduced by the Dutch of trimming trees and shrubs into grotesque shapes detracts from the pleasing effect, and gives a stunted, artificial character to the scene.

And here, again, we met with striking indications of that utter absence of modesty and that morbid craving for the obscene which is universal in Japan. Disgusting as such things are, it was impossible not to laugh at the devices to which

* *Incognito*, as applied to the progress of men of rank when travelling without their retinue.

a Yedo paterfamilias resorts, in his hours of domestic recreation, to amuse his wife and chil-dren, or the complete *abandon* with which these join in the sport, and endeavour to emulate the head of the family in his efforts to prove entertaining.

We breakfasted indoors, and it was very pleasant when, having done justice to the many good things provided for us, we stretch at full length on the soft clean mats, and look out drowsily on the blue sky, or at the winding brook as it ripples, beneath us, over its pebbly bed, or follow the vagaries of the gorgeous butterflies as they play among the bright flowers, and think what a beautiful thing this world of ours is, with a quiet sense of enjoyment such as men with an easy conscience and a full stomach only can feel.

Attendant moosmes—marvellously *coiffées* and *chaussés au naturel*, squat in the doorways; now one of them rises noiselessly, and on bended knee places a live coal before the extinguished cigar; now another advances, and fills the tiny egg-shell cup with fragrant amber-coloured tea.

Then they retire to their posts, watching, with their bright black eyes, the booted Tojins— silent, untiring servitors, ever ready to antici- pate and to minister to our wants.*

A sleepy, luxurious feeling, steals over us, as we lie there and watch the wreaths of smoke from our cigars as they rise and mingle with the pure air without; and we all hate the " spoony "

* I wish I could have completed my picture of luxurious repose at Ojee, by peopling a terrestrial paradise with a bevy of lovely and fascinating houris, in the poetical fashion of Sherard Osborn, or with the artistic licence of the illus- trator of Mr. Oliphant's book. I must confess, at the risk of destroying some agreeable delusions, that the moosmes of Ojee (like the women of Japan generally, as far as my expe- rience goes) are devoid of beauty of either form or feature, and that an intelligent and good-natured expression, and the display of brilliant teeth, are insufficient to redeem their numerous physical defects.

As regards the actual condition of the tea-house girls, I believe we are a good deal in the dark ; but whether they are, as some allege, paragons of virtue, or, as is believed by others, the most abandoned and profligate of their sex, certain it is that in the presence of Europeans their conduct is irreproach- able, and that any attempt at familiarity would be instantly checked and resented. It is strange how widely the ideal of beauty, as represented by Japanese artists, differs from the actual type, as my illustrations, copied from native paintings, will show.

who breaks the silence by declaring that whenever
he marries, he will pass his honeymoon at Ojee.
Why cannot he hold his stupid tongue, and let
us dream on, as we people the spot with dear
absent forms and faces, that now, alas! and for
many a weary day to come, we can see only in
our dreams?   For Ojee is a long way from
Pimlico, and my road to it lies through Pekin!

And as we lie there, at peace with all the
world and happy in our reveries, the clash of
arms and the groans of strong men in their
agony are heard in the streets of Yedo, and its
pavements are red with blood.

The scene changes from the pretty cottages
and green lanes of beautiful Ojee to the official
quarter of Yedo.

The Gotairo * had paid his ceremonial visit
to his royal nephew, and, borne in his norrimon
in the midst of a hundred armed retainers, he
had passed the outer moat and emerged into the

* Prince Regent, uncle to the Tycoon, and administering
the government during the latter's minority.

open space which lay between the Tycoon's palace and his own.

Yonder, on an eminence in the midst of a richly-wooded park, is his princely residence, and around the open gate—which, alas! poor Gotairo, thou shalt never pass in life—lounge his guards.

One of the main streets of Yedo leads into this space, and from that direction a group of men is seen approaching slowly. The morning has been showery, and they wear their wide-brimmed straw hats and rain-coats. They may be labourers going to their work, or traders, or Daimio's men—who knows?

Now, having reached the square, they halt, for the procession draws near, and all men must kneel as it passes.

Suddenly, as if by word of command, they cast off their rain-coats, and, glittering in coats of mail, their bright swords brandished on high, they spring upon the Gotairo, as, unconscious of danger, he reclines in his chair. His followers, unprepared for attack, stand aghast as one of the norrimon-bearers falls to the ground, cleft from

the skull to the chin. The norrimon lies a wreck
—there are shouts and groans—and then a man
rushes through the barrier, waving a bleeding tro-
phy, as he cries to the astounded guardian of the
gate, " Make way for the head of the Gotairo ! "

The assailed, if they could not save, will
avenge their chief. A furious conflict ensues :
the assassins are but one to five. Several lie
dead ; others, desperately wounded, have yet time
to commit the Hari Kari ; four are overpowered,
and reserved for a less sudden death : only
three cut their way through their enemies, and
escape.

Ten minutes later, and all is quiet. The
Gotairo's procession has passed into the palace ;
the dead and the wounded have disappeared as
if they had never been. A shower has washed
away the blood, and men, as they pass upon
their errands, do not stop to notice the fragments
of a norrimon, and beneath it the bleeding fingers
of a human hand. These are the only remaining
traces of the Gotairo's death.*

* The Abbé Girard, Interpreter to the French Consulate-
General, passed the execution ground, which adjoins the

On the following day the unfortunate officer
on duty at the barrier through which the murdered prince's head had been borne in triumph,
and who had failed to arrest the assassin, was
requested to perform the Hari Kari. He was a
highly-respectable and respected individual, and
a large party of his relations and friends assembled at his residence to witness the ceremony.
Having taken leave of them, and admitted the
justice of his sentence, he made a superficial
crucial incision on his abdomen with the small
knife worn for such emergencies, and then hand-
ing his large sword to his nearest male friend
(who stands on such occasions in the same relation as the best man at an English wedding),

high road to Kanagawa, a few days after these events,
and saw a man being burnt alive. He was reported to
be one of the murderers of the Gotairo. The three who
escaped managed to reach their homes in the dominions of
Prince Meto, but, some months afterwards, they were taken
after a desperate resistance. I saw them, tied hand and foot,
carried in a strong wooden cage through the streets of Kanagawa on their way to Yedo, in the dungeons of which they
would probably expiate their crime by the most horrible of
lingering deaths.

he bared and bent his neck ; the blade gleamed
in the air, fell, and the head rolled on the
ground.*

It may be imagined that such an event as the
murder of the Prince Regent, in open day and
in the public streets of the capital, must have
spread like wildfire, producing amazement and
consternation throughout the city ; yet, strange
to say, few appeared to be aware of it, and the
officers about the Legation when questioned said
that they had heard something about a fight
near the palace, but that the Gotairo was quite
well.

Mr. Alcock, on his making official inquiries,
was informed that it was true that the Gotairo
had been attacked and slightly wounded, but on
his offering his services in a surgical capacity (he
had studied and practised medicine with great
success in early life) met with a cold refusal.

---

* I believe the act of disembowelment never takes place
in these enlightened times : the crucial incision satisfies the
requirements of justice. The Hari Kari is viewed as an
indulgence, since it does not, like death by the hand of the
executioner, degrade the family of the victim.

To all his subsequent inquiries, as to those of his colleagues, the invariable reply was that the Gotairo was "neither better nor worse," which, considering that his head had not been recovered, was perfectly true; and six weeks elapsed before the representatives of foreign Powers were officially informed that the attack upon the Prince Regent had resulted in immediate death.

Extracts from my Diary.—April 29.—Visited Osakusa (pronounced Osaxa), the festive quarter of Yedo, and which reminds me, with differences, of Greenwich Fair, as it used to be in my boyhood.

Here the holiday makers disport themselves all the year round. Here are stalls with sweetmeats and fruits, toys, pictures, and all the wares likely to attract the multitude of men, women, and children. Here are booths in which wild beasts, giants, dwarfs, and every kind of wonder, are on exhibition. Here are theatres, peep-shows, and archery-grounds ; wrestlers, jugglers, dancing dogs, story-tellers, and puppet-shows.

In the midst of these grounds stands the cele-brated Temple of Quanon, a very large and rather imposing structure, with a solid portico in red lacquer. It is dedicated to a god given to equestrian exercise. In an adjoining street two milk-white horses are kept for his exclusive use. These animals, which we were allowed to inspect, have, we were told, never been mounted by man, and their only exercise consists in a daily walk through the temple grounds, so that when-ever the god feels disposed for a ride he will find them fat and sleek, though, I fear, like Japanese horses generally, a trifle puffed in the legs.

Within the temple there is little noteworthy, unless it be the gallery of portraits—not of saints, or priests, or martyrs, but of the principal cour-tesans of Yedo, whose forms and features are here immortalized *pour encourager les autres.*

They are wonderful pleasure-seekers, these Japanese. I suppose that there could not have been less than 10,000 or 12,000 people assem-bled in the grounds, and but for the aid of the Yaconins who attended us, we should never have been able to make our way through the

TEMPLE OF QUANON.

(From a Japanese Engraving on Copper.)

dense mass,* as its groups swayed to and fro in the pursuit of their various pleasures, or gathered around us in open-mouthed wonder. Occasionally, we met with the savage scowl of a flushed Daimio's follower, and, two or three times, angry cries of " Tojin ! " and " Baca ! " fell upon our ears; but the demeanour of the great mass was, if not friendly, certainly inoffensive. I do not know how far we had to thank our escort for this.

One of the great sights of Osakusa are the waxwork and carved wooden figures illustrative of Japanese character. They are of full size; and, as we all agreed, more lifelike, and in every respect superior to the best exhibition of the kind in Europe, Madame Tussaud's not excepted.†
So perfect, indeed, were some of these figures,

---

* The population of Yedo is estimated at 2,000,000, but this is, probably, an exaggeration.

† It is said that the practice of dissecting human bodies is strictly prohibited, under severe penalties, in Japan. It seems difficult to reconcile this with the perfection and symmetry of the representations of figures by the higher class of native artists, whether in painting or in carving, which indicate a sound knowledge of human anatomy.

that it actually required the sense of touch to convince us that we were not regarding flesh and blood. I had on several occasions seen the fair sex in Japan going through the different stages of their ablutions and dressings outside their street-doors; but I was now for the first time initiated into the real mysteries of their toilettes, and so wonderfully natural were these representations, that my innate modesty was most severely outraged. I felt as if I had strayed into forbidden ground, and as guilty as Peeping Tom of Coventry. Japanese ladies of rank evidently resort to extraordinary devices for maintaining all their charms in the highest state of preservation, and their maids certainly enjoy no sinecures.

From this exhibition, we proceeded to the theatre; a tolerably substantial building, with pit, boxes, and gallery, and a raised stage, curtained off as with us. The merits of the performance we could not, of course, appreciate; but a large audience testified their approval by loud and repeated shouts of laughter. The actors were a man, a woman, and a boy; and the pantomime was sufficiently expressive to demonstrate the plot of the piece. This turned upon the amours of a fat priest, who endeavoured by various means—by presents, threats, professions, serenades, and violence—to win the favour of a lady who, though coy, did not altogether disapprove of his attentions. Her son, a precocious *gamin*, given to practical jokes and somewhat indecent gestures, was the evil genius, and showed as little respect for his mother as for the priest. After various absurd love passages, in all of which the poor suitor is made a fool of, now tumbling from a ladder as he attempts to climb into his lady's chamber, now drenched with a basin of water as he serenades her under her window, or upset from a boat as he pursues her on the water, the heroine, with her scapegrace son, tired of his importunities, mounts a platform, and from thence stepping upon a rope extended across the theatre, they perform a *pas de deux*, the figures of which, if not graceful, are so expressive of contempt and derision, that the poor lover rends his garments in rage and depair, and the curtain falls

upon the moral that elderly priests should not
go galivanting after fair ladies.

The priest, like the pantaloon of our Christmas pantomimes, appears to be the *souffre dou-
leur* of the Japanese stage, and is generally a
prominent object in their caricatures.

On leaving the theatre, our Yaconins, who
had been highly pleased with the performance,
led us to an adjoining shed, where, instead of
the "regular drama," a travestie on the piece
we had just witnessed was being acted by
monkeys, admirably "got up" in the parts of
the priest, the lady, and the *enfant terrible*. The
poor animals had been carefully trained; and
so perfect were they in their pantomimic indecencies, that they only required speech to have
made them really formidable rivals to their two-
legged brothers and sisters next door.

May 16.—While at dinner to-day we were
alarmed by the sudden entrance of some Yaconins, who, with terror depicted in their faces,
cried "Cadgé! cadgé!" and pointed to some un-

seen danger without. Our first impulse was to arm ourselves against the meditated attack of a band of assassins ; but we were shortly relieved by finding that we were only threatened with being burnt out — a building adjoining my stables, in the immediate vicinity of the Consulate, having taken fire.

Nothing can exceed the perfect organization of a Japanese fire-brigade. A minute or two after the alarm had been given, two or three hundred men were on the spot, each taking up his allotted post and preparing to do the special duty devolving upon him. They were all dressed in the peculiar costume used only on these occasions, and were divided into different sections ; one carrying buckets of water, another ladders, a third long poles, with hooks attached, for demolishing buildings; and a fourth in charge of the engines, of which I noticed several descriptions made on European models. Each section was under the command of officers, who set their men an admirable example of activity and fearlessness, and clambered about the roofs of burning houses in spite of their two swords and baggy pantaloons, with the agility of cats.

Wood and paper form the materials of Japanese towns, and a fire accordingly spreads with incredible rapidity, leaving hardly a trace of habitation after the lapse of a few hours. The first object of the fire-brigades is, accordingly, to confine its ravages by demolishing adjoining buildings; on the premises where fires originate there is rarely time to save anything.

I trembled for my poor horses, who, startled by the unusual concourse, the shouts, the crackling of burning rafters, and the red glare of the fire, began to show symptoms of terror. If they broke loose what a general scrimmage there would be! But even that would be preferable to the more imminent danger of their being burnt alive. Fortunately, however, the night was calm, and through the exertions of that very efficient body, the Kanagawa fire-brigade, the devouring element, as the newspaper reporters will call it, was subdued before it had done any material mischief.

May 24.—To Yedo to join in the first cele-
bration of the Queen's birthday in Japan.
Speeches from M. de Bellecourt and Mr. Harris.
The latter informed us, *à propos de bottes*, that
Englishmen and Americans spoke the same
language, sprang from the same stock, and that
Shakspeare belonged to both of us. I think I
have heard something of the sort said before at
public dinners. Thirteen of us sat down to
table—an ominous number. Who will be the
victim this time? *

May 31.—Asked to Yedo to meet the Bishop
of Victoria; Lord Richard Grosvenor and Colonel
Shelley also there. After breakfast Itsojee, the
famous conjuror, was introduced, and performed
his best tricks; they have often been described,
and never better than by Sherard Osborn. The
butterfly trick is marvellous—certainly the most
graceful piece of legerdemain known. It is

* At the risk of being hooted, I confess to a weakness with
regard to this "vulgar superstition." I dare say poor Mr.
Euskin would have been murdered, even had he not been
one of our party, but——!

wonderful to see two scraps of common paper developing themselves into the form of butterflies,
gradually becoming endued with life and motion ;
at first faintly fluttering their wings, then,
gently rising, posed in mid air, and at length,
as if feeling their power, fairly taking flight and
enjoying their brief holiday existence, as now
they kiss the sweet-scented flowers; now daintily
sip water from a crystal bowl; now chase one
another through the air ; now rest side by
side, as if collecting strength for another excursion. The delusion is perfect. All this time
Itsojee sits calmly waving his fan ; and it is
not until its motion ceases that the butterflies
fall to the ground—mere scraps of whity-brown
paper.

We were all delighted; the Bishop has his
note-book out, and is busy making entries ; "all
done by the current of air produced by a fan,"
says his lordship, in an ecstacy of delight. I
venture to hint my suspicion that the butterfly
may possibly be attached to the handle of the
fan by a silken thread, but am sternly rebuked
for my scepticism and retire abashed, not, how-

ever, without a muttered, "*E pur se muove*"—
by means of a string!

And that reminds me that Galileo never uttered
such words; at least, according to modern wise-
acres, who take a malignant delight in destroying
one's pet illusions, and shaking one's faith in the
past.

People have actually taken the trouble to
write books to prove that Romulus was never
suckled by a wolf—that the first Cæsar never
wrote "*Veni, vidi, vici*"—that Nero never played
the fiddle while Rome was burning—that New-
ton never saw an apple fall—that our great
Duke never said, "Up, Guards, and at 'em!"
Why, we shall be told next, that Lord Panmure
never wrote his famous despatch, "Take care of
Dowb"!

Wherefore, I should like to know, do people
go out of their way to *désillusionner* (we have no
English word for it) their unoffending fellow-
creatures? The happiest children are those
who firmly believe in "Cinderella" and "Jack
the Giant-Killer," and men are but children of
a larger growth.

Still, I do assert, and I do not care who denies it, there *is* a connecting link of silk or hair between the butterfly and the fan of Itsojee.

The French Commander-in-Chief in China has lately sent over two officers of his staff, MM. de Cools and Montauban, to buy horses. The matter was one of some difficulty, as the Japanese Government had recently reduced the number to be sold to me to one thousand, on the plea that the country could not spare more. The French Consul-General now demanded that these officers should obtain the same number as had been promised to me, and, as is unfortunately too common with European diplomatists in the East, accompanied his demands with the hackneyed threat of striking his flag and going on board a French man-of-war (which, by the way, is a *rara avis* in Japanese waters) in the case of refusal.

I had a safe champion in Mr. Alcock, however, and he insisted that, on the "first come, first served" principle, my wants were to be supplied before those of our allies. Fortunately, my competitors in the horse-market were men of sense and discretion, and feeling, as we did, that we were working in a common cause, a compromise satisfactory to both parties was effected between us, to the discomfiture of the dealers, who had reckoned upon making a good thing out of our rivalry.

The shipping of my horses, which commenced in May, afforded intense delight to the Japanese, though the poor horses themselves did not seem to share in any such feeling. It was the first instance of equine emigration from Japan, and it required a good deal of persuasion to induce them to enter the lighters which were to bear them for ever from their native shores. The process of slinging, the novel voyage through the air as they were hauled on board, and the strange sights and smells, when at length secured in their stalls, completely bewildered them. They had yet to learn the horrors of sea-sickness. Could they have looked beyond, and foreseen what awaited them in China, from their being cast ashore on the muddy banks of Pehtang to their final disbandment and melancholy end in the shafts of a Chinese cart, they would certainly have committed suicide on the way.

I shall never forget the scene presented by one of my transports, the *Forest Eagle*, which sailed for China with above two hundred horses, in the beginning of June, and, after making barely three hundred miles in three weeks, returned into port disabled, with the remnant of her cargo.

The horses had all been stowed between decks, and a line of stalls, which had been constructed with as much strength as a Japanese carpenter could bestow upon them, having given way during a hurricane, the poor beasts, half maddened with fear and tortured by their hurts as they rolled among the fragments of their boxes, commenced an onslaught upon one another, which death or sheer exhaustion only terminated.

When the ship returned into harbour, only seventy horses survived, and of these several had had their eyes kicked out, or were otherwise so mutilated as to render their destruction necessary.

I may here mention that I never could prevail upon a Japanese to destroy a horse for the purpose of putting it out of its misery. I believe they would as soon cut a man's throat in cold blood. Even in cases of locked jaw they would let the poor beast linger in its agony, but, when all was over, they invariably laid a mat or rug decently over the carcase. Their respect for the dead seems to extend to the brute creation.

July 4.—A man convicted of having stolen some money from an European merchant at Yokuhama was executed to-day. From all I can learn, I am inclined to believe that the criminal code of Japan, though very severe, is administered with justice and impartiality, and that the system which prevails in China of allowing criminals under sentence of death to purchase a substitute, is unknown here.

Starting with the principle that every infraction of the law is a crime meriting death, it is but as a natural consequence that a scale of capi-

K

tal punishments, graduated in proportion to the offence, should be in force. If a man who steals to the value of ten kobangs* must be decapitated, he who turns traitor to his country, or sets fire to his neighbour's house, or murders his comrade, should surely meet with a more severe punishment. Inflictions of death, of a more or less painful or lingering nature, preceded in extreme cases by various modes of torture, are therefore resorted to, less from cruelty than from a rude sense of justice.

The great fêtes of the year take place in July, and business is banished for a while. Disconsolate European merchants prowl around the closed gates of the Custom-house of Yokuhama, vainly hoping to find some good-natured official ready to sacrifice his holiday in order to change their dollars or grant them permits for landing or shipping goods. But, alas! there is the notice, under the hand and seal of the Consuls, that for this day and two days to come no business will be transacted. The shops are closed, and garlands

---

* Thefts below that amount are by a recent law not punishable with death.

of flowers are hung across the streets. Every house is decorated, and on this particular occasion the decorations are not of a kind to bear inspection. The roads are crowded with country-people pouring in to enjoy their holiday, and all the sights and shows of Osakusa appear to have been transported for the nonce to Yokuhama.

A religious character—if the word may be applied without irreverence to such orgies—is attached to these fêtes, and the priests take a prominent part in the various processions which perambulate the streets.

One of these was peculiarly characteristic of Japan. It was composed of the public women of Yokuhama performing their annual pilgrimage to a temple in the vicinity under the guidance of their spiritual instructors, who, clad in gorgeous robes, headed the *cortège*. Virgins (the eldest could not have been more than ten years of age) brought up the rear, while officials marched on the flanks, bearing aloft emblems which, if decidedly inconsistent with our ideas of decency, were not altogether inappropriate to the occasion.

Arrived at the temple, the ladies performed their devotions with the most perfect propriety of demeanour, passed their hands reverently over the wooden image of their particular deity, prayed for success and prosperity in their *métier*, and returned to the Gankeroo, quits with the past and hopeful for the future, in the happy, calm frame of mind of a *dévote* leaving the confessional.

Riding on the Nagasaki road the other day, I met with another striking illustration of the entire absence of modesty which astonishes Europeans on their first visits to Japan. A little urchin, seated at the door of a neat and substantial dwelling-house, gave the alarm of the approach of a Tojin, and as I passed I had the pleasure of seeing the whole family rush into the street to gaze at me. Although unaccustomed to the contemplation of ladies and gentlemen literally *décolletés jusqu'à la jarretière*, I retained my presence of mind sufficiently to notice that this family group represented three generations. There were two very old women; one unmistakable old man; then Paterfamilias with his wife; lastly, some half-dozen boys and girls, from about eighteen to six years of age. They were all *stark naked*, and, to all appearance, perfectly unconscious of the fact, as they stared at me in open-eyed wonder. After having passed some little distance, I looked back; they were still at their doors quietly chatting, and, I suppose, criticising my appearance. I wondered whether they would dress for dinner.

How are we to account for these things? Some enthusiastic admirers of Japan insist that this absence of shame is the natural result of perfect primitive innocence, and that the Japanese are really as little aware that they are naked as Adam and Eve were before the Fall. But, alas! we know too well that they have long since tasted of the forbidden tree; nay, eaten so heartily that scarcely a single fruit remains to tempt their appetites. So far from being unconscious of evil, we unfortunately know that their most innocent pleasures are sys-

tematically tarnished with obscenity and licen-
tiousness.

It is just credible that a state of society might
exist, in which purity of morals should not be
inconsistent with a disregard of what the lovers
of primitive nature might term the conventional
laws of modesty ; but such a state of society has
never been in Japan.   There the people are not
innocent of wrong, but, on the contrary, glory in
outraging what they know to be right.   Nor is
theirs the modesty of the Turkish woman, who
drew her only garment over her head to hide the
blushes of her cheek at the expense of the rest
of her person.   The Japanese are depraved, sen-
sual, and obscene in every sense.   The men of
all classes—from the first Daimio in the land to
the meanest of his retainers—delight in contemplating human nature in its most animal form.
Respectable mothers of families, and young girls
of otherwise irreproachable conduct, will take an
undisguised pleasure in sights and scenes which
would shock an English street-walker ; and little
innocent-eyed children, toddling by their fond
father's side, or nestling in their mother's bosom,

may be seen playing with toys so indecent, that one longs to dash them from their tiny hands and trample them under foot.*

Yet, co-existing with this state of things, we find woman occupying a high social position in Japan. Among the labouring classes she is neither the beast of burden, nor the domestic drudge, but the respected helpmate of her lord, taking her proper place as the mistress of his family and household. In a class above this she is equally on a footing with her husband, whether

---

* In shopping in Japan, the greatest care must be exercised to guard against the acquisition of indecencies which are found not only in books and pictures, but are painted on their porcelain, embossed on their lacquer, carved in their ivory, and surreptitiously conveyed into their fans. Mr. Alcock made a purchase of illustrated books destined for some children in England, and it was only by a fortunate accident that he discovered among them, before they were de-spatched, pictures which would have disgraced Holywell Street. I was deeply grieved to learn that even the sacred character of the Bishop of Victoria, who had neglected the precaution of minute examination, could not save him from a similar outrage. Had not an acquaintance providentially examined his porcelain cups, they would, in all probability, have been stopped and confiscated at the English Custom House as inadmissible, even as the private property of a bishop.

tending his children, with a full authority over all pertaining to home, or assisting him in his business, with discretionary powers to act on his behalf. I have been informed, on excellent authority, no less than that of a married man, that henpecked husbands are by no means rare in Japan.

Of the higher ranks of women I cannot speak, never, I grieve to say, having had the honour of forming their acquaintance ; but I am led to believe that the rights of woman, within proper limits, of course, are perfectly understood and admitted by men of rank.*

I think I am also safe in asserting that, whatever may have been a woman's antecedents, breaches of chastity on the part of wives, are very rare, which is not surprising when we bear in mind that the penalty of a *faux pas* is death to the offenders and irremediable disgrace to those connected with them. If a breach of the

---

* This opinion gains confirmation from the fact that women have wielded and may again wield the sceptre of the Mikado. How trying for ladies, never being allowed to wear any article of dress a second time!

marriage vow were, with us, punished by the decapitation of the lady and her paramour, the self-immolation of the injured husband, and the ruin and degradation of the relatives of all concerned, Sir Cresswell Cresswell's post would soon become a sinecure.

It must, however, be taken into account that Japanese husbands, while allowing themselves the widest licence, take the precaution of preventing their wives being led astray by a love of admiration.

Whatever beauty a Japanese woman possesses is in her eyes, her expression, and her teeth. The effect of the two former is effectually marred by the practice, to which all wives must needs submit, of shaving off the eyebrows, which gives a peculiarly vacant and idiotic cast to the countenance; while the sweetest smile in the world becomes abortive when accompanied by the display of a row of black lacquered teeth, which process is another of the trifling drawbacks on domestic happiness in Japan. It is, no doubt, a very reprehensible, dog-in-the-manger kind of feeling which prompts a husband to render his wife so unattractive, and it borders, moreover, on what is vulgarly called " cutting off one's nose to spite his face"; for the morning contemplation of the wife of his bosom, as with lips half parted, she slumbers by his side, cannot be agreeable to him under such circumstances; but, no doubt, it is effectual in keeping away those young gallants who, all the world over, are found anxious and ready to disturb the peace of mind of poor husbands.

While on this subject, I may record a domestic tragedy which was related to me, by one of the Government interpreters, as of very recent occurrence.

The young and beautiful wife of a powerful Daimio was left, as usual, to pass the period of her lord's retirement to his dominions, in the privacy of his palace in Yedo. A gay Lothario, attached in some capacity or other to the household, availed himself of the husband's absence to fall in love with her, and, in spite of her teeth, to importune her with his illicit addresses, which she, as a well-conducted wife should do, rejected with scorn. Whether it were

that her refusal hurt his pride, or that it fired
his love, he became desperate, and at length succeeded in accomplishing by force what persuasion
failed to yield him.

The unconscious Daimio, on his return to
Yedo, flew, as in duty bound, to the arms of
his beloved, but she, repelling his embrace, told
him that she was no longer worthy to be called
his wife, and, although guiltless in intent, that
death alone could expiate her disgrace.

So saying, she drew her sword (ladies of rank
are allowed the privilege of bearing arms), and
plunged the blade into her body.

The fate of the villain was not known; the
unhappy husband committed the Hari Kari
with the entire approval of his son and heir and
assembled family.

But while chastity on the part of wives is
rarely infringed, unmarried women are subjected
to few restraints, nor does it appear that the
grossest profligacy disqualifies them for marriage.
That the nobles, as Europeans have reported,
resort to houses of ill-fame for the choice of
wives, I do not believe; I have heard, on the

contrary, that very great importance is attached to influential alliances between the families of the Daimios; but, it is certainly true, that men of good repute and consideration frequently marry tea-house girls, whose mode of life, if not calculated to teach them the household virtues, is supposed to have well fitted them for the management of an establishment.

I have said before that the actual condition of these girls is not well known : I never could get any reliable information on the subject. It appears certain, however, that they are generally the daughters of poor people who, unable to provide for them by other means, apprentice them out at a tender age as attendants at tea-houses, where they are taught their business in all its branches. These houses are under the control of the Government, whose officers regulate their interior economy, and which participates in the profits. After a certain age, the apprentices, unless conditions to the contrary should have been made, can be purchased outright or hired for a stipulated period, through the intervention of public officials.

That most candid of charlatans, Mr. Barnum, tells us in his memoirs, that the real genuine mermaid, which he exhibited in his museum at New York to admiring thousands, was obtained from ' a Yankee ship-captain, who reported having procured it in Japan.

In the course of a shopping tour in Yokuhama, I came across several specimens of the same kind, and I had puzzled over them for a long time, utterly at a loss to reconcile their strange incongruities, partaking, as they did, of man, beast, fowl, and fish, before I discovered, or rather suspected—for discovery required a dissecting process—that this *lusus naturæ* was ingeniously manufactured, by the hand of man, out of a composition of paper, pulp, leather, and glue.

The shopkeeper, who dealt principally in livestock, dogs, chickens, singing-birds, &c., did not attempt to deny the ingenious fraud when taxed with it, but assured me that he sold a great many to the Funi-Yaconins (ship-captains), who never doubted his word when he assured them that the nondescripts had been caught in the interior of Japan.

There is rather a rage for Japanese dogs at present, but I do not admire them; they are evidently descendants of the Blenheim breed of spaniels, but have degenerated considerably from the ancestral stock. They are valued in proportion to their diminutiveness and shortness of nose, and are the favourite pets and extravagance of ladies of rank.

Of poultry, as of the feathered tribe generally, I am, to my shame be it said, very ignorant; I am told, however, that there are in Japan many specimens as yet unknown in England. A small, game-looking chicken, with his feathers reversed, like a silk hat brushed the wrong way, is much prized; I think it must be unmatched in ugliness.

My friend of the mermaid had also a fair collection of pheasants, but no varieties that do not exist in Europe.*

---

* I subsequently discovered a specimen, of which I sent a skin to the secretary of the Zoological Society in London, who states that it does not exist in England, but is known by description as "Temmenick's" Pheasant, so called after its first discoverer, a Dutch naturalist.

Extract from Diary, August 22.—" *Camilla* sails to-morrow on Commissariat affairs, for Hakodadi. I was to have gone in her, but, detained by business, sent B—— in my place. On board to say good-bye to Colvile, who is in low spirits at being kept away from the seat of war ; so am I. He is also vexed at losing our promised trip to Fusi-jama, but is to call and pick us up at some place on the coast, where Mr. Alcock intends to take the sulphur baths."

Poor Colvile ! I never saw him again. He made a good passage, and left Hakodadi, to return, on the 2nd September. He must have had bad weather at starting, and on the 9th is supposed to have foundered in one of the fiercest typhoons that ever raged in these waters. But for some accidental difficulty about one of my horse transports, which rendered my absence inexpedient, I should have accompanied him and shared his fate, and that of his gallant officers and crew. We were much together, and I had the greatest regard and esteem for him.

The Japanese, although as a race little given to the outward observances of their religion, are yet a superstitious race, and their organ of veneration is strongly developed. They despise their priesthood, as a body of mendicants who, living in idleness and sloth, fatten upon the industry and thrift of their more energetic brethren; but they yet cling tenaciously to the gods and the traditions of their forefathers. And this feeling will ever prove a more serious stumbling-block to the efforts of Christian missionaries than all the prohibitory laws of the State or the impotent denunciations of the priesthood.

If there is one sentiment universal among all classes of Japanese, it is a deep and earnest reverence for their sacred mountain Fusi-jama—the temple, the grave, and the monument of the father of their faith.*

Two hundred centuries are supposed to have elapsed since, created by a convulsion of nature

* Sin-fuh, whose doctrines may be considered to represent, with regard to the various forms of the Buddhist faith in Japan, much the same relative position as the Roman Catholic Church occupies towards other Christian Churches in Europe.

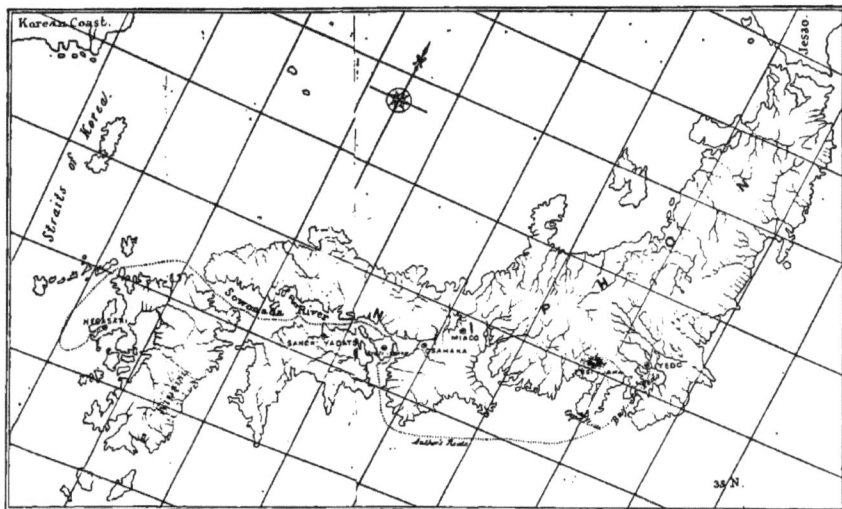

OUTLINE OF A MAP OF JAPAN
Showing the Route through the Seurmade Sea
Reduced from an Original Japanese Map.

Scale or 200 Miles

in a single night, Fusi-jama reared its proud crest and challenged the worship and the love of the millions who, from the extremest ends of the island, gazed with awe and devotion upon its snowy peak as it glittered for the first time in the morning sun, or faded into the mist of evening. And this reverence has survived time and change; has grown with the growth and strengthened with the strength of the Japanese people. Fusi-jama is their ideal of the beautiful in nature, and they are never weary of admiring, glorifying, and reproducing it. It is painted, embossed, carved, engraved, lacquered, modelled on all their wares; men carry it in their pockets, women wear it on their persons, and children by the roadside build miniature Fusi-jamas of mud, as our own make dirt-pies. It must be allowed that, next to the obscene, there is nothing that the Japanese so much love to represent as the beautiful; fruits and flowers, birds and butterflies,* gliding rivers and rushing cataracts are ever favourite subjects

* Unfortunately, the beauties of these are external only; the birds, so gorgeous in their plumage, are voiceless; the fruits, so luscious to the eye, are tasteless; the flowers, so rich and varied in form and colour, are scentless. The ill-natured say that the latter want is more than supplied by the people.

of the painters, and, prominent among these, you ever find their beloved mountain. The Daimio will stop his norrimon, the peasant will lean upon his spade, the fisherman will drop his oar, the coolie will lay down his burden, to gaze upon it and worship it in his heart. Nay, I have seen a business-like official at the Custom-house forget his duty and his dignity to call the foreigner's attention to its beauties under some peculiar light.

Fancy a London tidewaiter dropping the lid of your unsearched portmanteau, while, in an ecstacy of enthusiastic delight, he points out the effect of a straggling sunbeam on the dome of St. Paul's!

While all share in the admiration, it may be doubted whether they partake alike in the religious associations connected with Fusi-jama, or in the perfect confidence with which the mass of the people view it, not only as the shrine of their dearest gods, but the certain panacea for their worst evils, from impending bankruptcy or cutaneous diseases, to unrequited love or ill luck at play. The annual pilgrimage is, accordingly, performed by thousands upon thousands. If attended with beneficial results, the gods are

GODS OF FUSI-JAMA.

F.G. Nethercleft, Sc.

praised and Fusi-jama is glorified; if otherwise, the pilgrim has the melancholy satisfaction to know that his own sins are at fault and require further expiation.

Men of rank never take part in these pilgrimages, and women are only allowed to do so once in every sixty years.*

Mr. Alcock had long wished to exercise his right of travelling in the interior of the country, and a visit to Fusi-jama, besides promising to be of extreme interest, offered the best possible pretext for an expedition. The authorities, of course, made innumerable objections, and proved the utter and entire impossibility of such an undertaking being accomplished; but Mr. Alcock was pretty well accustomed to such arguments, and having successfully disposed of all the " insuperable obstacles," left Yedo for Fusi-jama on the 3rd of September.

His party was composed of Messrs. Eusden, Gower, and Macdonald, members of the Legation; Lieutenant Robinson, of the Indian navy;

* Their turn came last year (1861), and, to judge from the enormous number of pilgrims, their grievances must be many.

Mr. S. Gower, Mr. Veitch, a botanist, and myself.*

One of the Vice-Governors of Yedo, Matabé,
the interpreter to the Legation, and several Yaconins, formed our escort, and norrimon-bearers,
bettos, coolies, servants, and followers, together
with a troop of pack-horses, swelled our *cortège*
to the dimensions of a small invading army.

Mr. Alcock, although he had of necessity
asked the Japanese Government to make arrangements for our comfort and security *en route*, had
stipulated that he should be as little as possible
embarrassed by the presence of officials, as he
wished to travel *niebon*.   There was none of the
state, accordingly, with which a Japanese functionary of any rank would have surrounded himself in his progress; and instead of being borne
in norrimons, the only conveyance used by
Japanese gentlemen on similar occasions, we
travelled on horseback, a sacrifice of dignity to
comfort, which, however much it may have as-

---

* My account of our visit to Fusi-jama was published in
the *Times* shortly after the event.   It is now republished
with only a few alterations and additions.

tonished the natives, was an immense relief to our minds and our bodies.

VISIT TO FUSI-JAMA.

As may be imagined, the projected pilgrimage excited no small interest amongst the Japanese, who, as they crowded the streets of Kanagawa to watch our departure, seemed puzzled whether most to admire our temerity or marvel -.t our impudence. Some of the older men shook their heads ominously, declaring that no good could come to us or to their country from such a desecration of their gods; but the majority of the people were simply amused. They have seen and learnt so much within the last year that nothing can surprise them.

Our route, as far as Odawara, a distance from Yedo of about forty-five miles, was by the great highway to Nagasaki, skirting the sea. This is an admirable, broad, well-paved road, flanked on

both sides with gigantic cedars and limes, affording a most grateful shade from the still-powerful
sun.   The effect of many miles of these avenues
formed of trees averaging from 150 to 180 feet
in height, is very striking.

At Odawara we turned into the interior, and
commenced to cross the Hakoni Mountains, a
range running north and south between the sea-
shore and Fusi-jama.   Arrived at the summit,
after an eight-hours' march, we found ourselves
at a height which we computed about 6000 feet
above sea level, on the borders of a glassy lake,
six miles in length and one and a quarter in width.
Wonderful tales are related by the Japanese of
this lake, evidently of volcanic origin, which
they state to be bottomless in the centre and inhabited by an evil spirit, very much given to drag
unwary mortals below.   It was probably from
fears for our safety that no persuasion could induce our officers to procure us a boat to explore
these waters.

On the following morning we commenced our
descent from Hakoni, and on the evening of the
next day, the sixth from our departure, reached
Muri-jama, a village lying at the foot of the

mountain, and about 100 miles distant from Yedo. Here the authority of the Tycoon ceases, and spiritual government begins, the Holy Mountain being under the sole jurisdiction of the priesthood, two of which respectable body now attached themselves to our party, and never left us till we returned in safety to the foot of the mountain.

On the next day we rode about six miles to a place called Hashi-Mondo, where the steep ascent commences, and here, leaving our horses and equipping ourselves with pilgrims' staves, which the priests dispose of for the sum of one penny each, we girded up our loins and climbed manfully up the rugged and precipitous path, our light baggage being carried by Goliks, or "men of great vigour," a description which the appearance of these poor creatures, who earn their livelihood as beasts of burden to the pilgrims, did not by any means justify.

HEAD-QUARTER STAFF ENCAMPED AT FUSI-JAMA.

At every half-mile along the path a hut is erected, where pilgrims repose and are refreshed with cups of doubtful tea. During our six-hours' ascent we passed nine of these resting-places, and, darkness coming on, we took up our abode in the last, ate a modest dinner, and, stretching our weary limbs upon straw mats, slept as well as the cold and the fleas would allow us.

THE STORMING OF FUSI-JAMA.

We had now accomplished over two-thirds of the ascent, but the worst was yet to come. Hitherto the path, though steep and rugged, had afforded a tolerably firm foothold ; but the rest of the way was over loose pieces of lava, scoria, and cinders, and at every few yards the ascent became more precipitous. It was curious to remark how some of our party, who had before shown themselves somewhat insensible to the beauties of nature, would now stop every few minutes to admire the scenery, generally seating themselves to do so; but some allowance must be made in consideration of the rarified state of the atmosphere, which rendered violent exercise somewhat difficult and made us gasp very painfully. At first, we met with little snow, but as we advanced we found large patches here and there, and on reaching the summit, after four hours' toil, the tubs of water near the temple were frozen into a compact mass. Still, the cold was not anything like what we had been led to suppose it would be, the thermometer at mid-day showing only 54° in the shade, and the mercury boiling at 186°.

The temple of Fusi-jama is a modest, unpretending little hut, adorned with a few gods in lava, and some common tinsel ornaments. Here the devout lay their offerings upon the altar, and in return have their garments stamped with strange figures and devices in token of their having accomplished their pilgrimage. Great virtue is attached to these stamps, particularly for the cure of cutaneous diseases, and their number is only limited by the size of the garment and the extent of the fee. I invested an entire uzeboo (eighteen pence), and received in return the impress of all the gods, and (unless likenesses are very deceptive), all the devils, too, of Fusi-jama.

Having sufficiently recovered breath, we proceeded to climb to the highest point of the crater, where Mr. Alcock's standard-bearer unfurled the British flag, while we fired a royal salute from our revolvers in its honour, and concluded the ceremony by drinking the health of Her gracious Majesty in champagne, iced in the snows of Fusi-jama.

The crater of Fusi-jama is between two and

three nautical miles in circumference, and about 600 yards in depth, and it resulted from observations made by Mr. Robinson that the highest point is rather more than 14,000 feet above the sea level. The Japanese have generally quoted it as 17,000.* The volcano is, and has been for centuries, perfectly extinct.

We were fortunate enough to have a fine, clear, sunny day for the ascent, and, as we looked below and around us, we beheld the fair land of Japan like a highly-coloured map, the points of its headlands jutting sharply into the blue sea, range upon range of mountains stretching across the full length of the island as far as the eye could reach, and rivers winding through green valleys, gradually increasing in size till they were lost in the sea. That one view would have richly repaid us for ten times our toil. Well may the Japanese be proud of their beautiful Fusi-jama!

The descent was comparatively easy, and, of

---

* Latitude, as taken from Peak of Fusi-jama 25° 31′ N.
  Longitude . . . . . . 138° 42′ E.
  Variation of compass . . . 3° 02′ W.

course, every one said at least once, *Facilis descensus*, &c., as we turned homewards, by a new and, if possible, finer route, till on the 15th we

DESCENT OF FUSI-JAMA.

reached Atamé, a picturesque village on the seashore, celebrated for its sulphur springs, whence I returned to Kanagawa by water, leaving Mr. Alcock and some of his party to take the baths.

I have so far confined myself to a bare description of our progress; I must now endeavour
to give some idea of the beauty of the country
which we traversed. As a tolerably old traveller
through all quarters of the globe, I can speak
with some authority, and I do not hesitate to
say that the scenery which gladdened our eyes
and hearts during the journey to and from Fusi-
jama cannot be equalled within the same compass in any part of the world. Its great charm,
probably, lies less in its intrinsic beauty than in
its continually-varying character. The eye has
never time to weary. Now you are in a noble
avenue of majestic trees (and no tree is finer
than the cedar of Japan—*Cryptomeria Japonica*);
suddenly you emerge into an open country,
among cornfields and flowering shrubs; then
you plunge into a deep forest; then again you
find yourself in a perfectly English green lane,
with honeysuckle on the hedges and daisies on
the banks, and in the distance, embosomed in
trees and shrubs of the brightest foliage, groups
of the most picturesque little white cottages in
the world. You have barely time to dream of

home when you are once more transported into a rugged mountain path, with torrents roaring at your feet, and as you reach its height there lies the broad blue sea on one side, while on the other Fusi-jama rises majestically from its broad base. I doubt whether, if all the most wild, lovely, rich, and magnificent views in the world could be collected and formed into a group, they would produce a finer picture.

Throughout, the vegetation is most luxuriant. From the deepest valley to the mountain-tops, you behold one dense mass of flowering shrubs and trees, in the foliage of which there is as great a variety as in the scenery.

The land is generally well cultivated, rice and millet forming the principal crops in the districts through which we passed. We came across small patches of cotton and tobacco here and there. Of tea we saw very little. Vegetables and fruits of all kinds grow in abundance.* I was particularly struck, however, with the almost entire absence of animal life during our progress. With the exception of the poultry

* See Appendix, No. 1.

and dogs in the villages, and a few pack-horses on the road, we hardly met a single specimen of the brute creation. No cattle, no sheep, no singing-birds, and, though we promised ourselves some shooting, not a symptom of game of any description. The Japanese assured us, however, that the mountains beyond Fusi-jama abounded in bears, wolves, wild ponies, deer, and boar.

The arrangements made by the Japanese Government for our accommodation *en route* left us nothing to wish for. Our halting-places had been arranged beforehand, and everything was ready prepared for our reception when we arrived. It was not considered becoming to allow the British Envoy to occupy a common tea-house, and we were accordingly accommodated in the houses specially reserved for the Daimios when on their travels. These were scrupulously clean, and provided always with bath-rooms and ample supplies of water.

As Mr. Alcock did not choose to travel in his official capacity, the authorities could not formally receive him at the different towns; but on our entrance we were invariably met by an escort of officers, who accompanied us to the full extent of their precincts ; and at Odawara the prince of that name, a very powerful Daimio, sent a deputation to welcome the English Minister to his dominions, and to wish him a pleasant journey.

The conduct of the people was excellent. The sight of eight mounted Englishmen must have appeared wonderful to them, who had never before beheld an European ; but they never once allowed their curiosity to become offensive, far less were they ever guilty of the slightest disrespect. As we entered their towns or villages (and these consist of one long street, sometimes three miles in length) men, women, and children, flocking out of their doors, appeared to present a dense, impervious wall to check our progress. But there is a quiet elderly gentleman in long petticoats, and a straw hat, tied under his chin, who precedes our *cortège* armed with a fan, and before a wave of this fluttering emblem of authority the enormous crowd falls back with far more alacrity and readiness than an English mob under similar circumstances could be got to do through the agency of Sir Richard Mayne and his legions, even if backed by a troop of Life Guards. Nor do they, like other mobs, close in our rear; but, remaining squatted at their doors, they watch us out of sight. In no case, whether escorted or alone, did we meet with a single instance of rudeness or incivility on the part of the people; nor did we, during the whole course of our journey, meet either a beggar or a drunken man.* The general appearance of the populace is one of great prosperity and contentment; their houses are remarkably clean and in good repair; their patches of garden well cultivated, and never without regard to ornament; and if they are not overburdened with clothing, it is evident that their will and not their poverty consents to forego this luxury. Would to Heaven we might travel as far in European countries—nay, even in our own favoured land, without meeting more misery!

We believe that the Japanese Government is

---

* Mendicancy, in any form, is contrary to law—though, in some few instances, cripples obtain a licence to beg. As a rule, every Daimio is responsible for the maintenance of the poor or disabled of his own dominions.

an oppressive one, yet it is difficult to reconcile such belief with the evident prosperity that prevails. No Eastern people is so free from the stamp of the slave as the Japanese. Let them bow their heads in the dust before a Yaconin as they may, it is less an act of servile submission than a courtesy exacted by usage and a duty owing to superior authority. Freedom is older than despotism; and centuries of arbitrary government have not extinguished its spark in the breast of the Japanese peasant. Those well-built, muscular men, who stand erect at their doors, holding their little children by the hand, have a sense of liberty and self-respect never to be met with in a race of slaves or cowards; those laughing women beside them know and appreciate the sacred happiness of the domestic hearth; even the little children (and nowhere do you meet this true indication of material prosperity—troops of merry, rosy-cheeked children—to a greater extent), even they do not crouch before the foreigner, though, doubtless, for many a day to come, they will, in their naughty moods, be threatened with the most terrible of Bogies—the *Tojins*.

On our arrival at Atamé, than which a more lovely little sea-coast town does not exist on the face of the earth, we were not met, as we had hoped, by the *Camilla* (she had, it is now supposed, been lost five days before this, on the 9th September), but H.M.S. *Berenice* (Indian navy), by which we received our English mails.

By an odd coincidence, on our opening the papers we found, in a late number of *Once a Week*, an article by Sherard Osborn, on "The Pilgrimage to Fusi-jama." Of course, we swaggered a good deal over it, and pitied his ignorance, and wondered how a man who had never been there could presume to write on the subject, misleading the public, &c., &c., &c.

Nevertheless, we remained in ignorance of the true meaning of "Fusi-jama," which Sherard Osborn and other writers (who have never been there, and, consequently, cannot know anything about it!) choose to translate, "the matchless mountain." That "jama" means mountain, we know; but no Japanese would allow that "fusi" meant matchless. One of our party declared that, on the contrary, "fusi" or "fusee" might

M 2

mean match-full, or full of matches, in allusion
to its volcanic nature; while another (who had
passed the Civil Service Examination), maintained Sherard Osborn's interpretation, suggesting that as "jama" undoubtedly means a
mountain, *Fusi*-jama must mean "Few-see a
mountain" (like it), which implies that it is un-
equalled or matchless. I fear the problem is
not yet satisfactorily solved.*

Shortly after my return to Kanagawa, I received the news of the fall of the Taku Forts,
with orders to break up my establishments in
Japan, and join the expeditionary army in the
north of China.

A few days later, Admiral Hope wrote, requesting that, as the war might now be considered at an end, I would dismiss my fleet of
transports, composed of no less than thirteen
steamers and sailing-vessels, and direct them to
proceed to Shanghae to be paid off.

Before all my arrangements had been com-

* See Appendix, No. 2.

pleted, the news reached us of the treacherous capture of our officers under a flag of truce, and their subsequent murder by slow torture; of the advance of the army on Pekin, the destruction of the Summer Palace, and the signing of the treaty.

The war was over; the Chinese had done their worst, and run to kennel; and being at our mercy, had been pleased to accept, with the worst possible grace, the easiest possible terms. Ambassadors and generals announced to the world their diplomatic and military victories; red ribbons and *grand cordons* were distributed, the genius of commanders was weighed in the scale of public opinion, and not found wanting; and yet English tax-payers were brutal enough to grumble at being required to contribute the trifling sum of six millions sterling, towards all these glories and successes!

It was with real regret that, towards the end of October, I bade farewell to the fair shores of Japan and the good friends I left behind me. This is not the place to acknowledge personal obligations, but I must not take my last look at

the green banks of fair Kanagawa and the old
familiar hill at the foot of which I had passed
the greater part of my ten months' residence,
without a grateful thought for Howard Vyse—
ever kind, considerate and unselfish—and, in
spite of his military administration of consular
law, no unworthy representative of English
manliness and honour; as is sufficiently testified
by the respect in which he is universally held
by his countrymen, and the unusual regard
entertained, by the Japanese of all classes, for
" the Consul with the big heart."

Partly to escape the prevailing head-winds,
partly to gratify my curiosity and extend my
experiences of Japan, I had arranged to proceed
to Nagasaki (where my duties required that I
should touch on my way to China), by the
great inland sea of Sowonada (I refer the reader
to a sketch of it); and, having obtained the
services of an experienced Japanese pilot, we
steamed away in the *Berenice* on the 22nd
October.

SOWONADA SEA

From my Diary.—October 24.—Entered the Sowonada Seas by a narrow passage called So-mara Sami, the banks of which are armed with a formidable-looking battery, completely commanding the entrance ; but from their being entirely exposed in rear (there are most convenient landing-places for an attacking party on the coast about two miles off), incapable of proving a serious obstacle.

Outside, the weather had been boisterous, and a heavy mist hung over the scene ; the contrast was the more striking, therefore, when, from the stormy sea, whose waves furiously lashed the wild, rugged coast, we suddenly passed into the unrippled waters,. with their quiet green banks and smiling villages, basking amid a rich and unbroken mass of verdure, in the bright morning sunshine.

Towards the afternoon, we reached the Bay of Osahaka (shortly to be opened to European commerce), and approached sufficiently close to this Japanese Liverpool, to be able to distinguish the great extent of the town, and the quantity of shipping in its harbour.

Hiogo, the site intended for European residents, is about six miles from Osahaka on the eastern side of the bay. Here we anchored for the night, our captain not being willing to run the risk of proceeding in the dark, with no better guide than a Japanese pilot and a worthless Admiralty chart.

25th.—Under way at daylight. As we proceed, the scenery increases in beauty as in variety. Lovely as were many of the scenes during my late trip to Fusi-jama, these far surpass them. I feel satiated with beauty, and yet never tire of gazing; for the landscape does not weary with sameness, but changes at every mile of our progress, " from grave to gay, from lively to severe," but always beautiful. Lago Maggiore, multiplied by a hundred, and a thousandfold diversified, could not surpass it in loveliness or grandeur. Perreau* appears completely overcome by it; he sits, with his sketch-book open, and, like a school-

---

* Lieutenant Perreau, of the 47th B.N.I. who was temporarily attached to me in Japan, and whom I have to thank for the greater part of the sketches in this book, as well as for his agreeable companionship.

INSIDE SOVON ▸

boy with unlimited credit in a pastrycook's shop, is puzzled where to begin. Anchored for the night at Sanoki Tadatso, a picturesque little town, with an admirably-constructed harbour of refuge, and a dock-yard of considerable dimensions.

It was tantalizing not to be able to land, but Mr. Alcock had particularly requested that we should abstain from doing so. We certainly received little encouragement from the population, who kept carefully aloof from us; even the fishermen's boats, with which we would gladly have transacted business, gave us as wide a berth as if we had the plague on board.

26th.—The scenery still improves; and as we progress the charts become more and more incorrect. According to the Admiralty, we crossed a range of mountains this morning; breakfasted in the middle of an enormous rice-field; passed the greater part of the day in an excursion through the interior, and anchored for the night about twenty miles inland in the midst of a dense forest.

We relied upon the lead and the pilot, however. For some time to-day our course lay between a long, curiously-shaped range of rocks of basaltic formation, on one side, and the high road

OUR PILOT.

between Yedo and Nagasaki, forming for many miles a straight unbroken avenue of magnificent maples and cedars, on the other. Suddenly we found ourselves in a little landlocked harbour, with an outlet so narrow that a pistol-shot would reach either bank; then we emerged into a wide expanse, studded with islands, so rich, so green, so inviting, that Perreau declares that he could make up his mind, if a certain somebody else would only be of his way of thinking, to pass his life here. Everywhere, from the water's edge to the mountain-tops, the vegetation is luxuriant; peace and prosperity seem to reign supreme, and the beauty of the scene is enhanced by the pure, unclouded, blue sky, reflected in the clear waters, and the grateful sunshine, which seems to linger here beyond its time, as if loth to leave the spot most worthy of its love.

Here and there along the banks, and more particularly at the narrower passages, batteries may be seen, half masked by trees and shrubs. They are right to hide their black muzzles; what business have the implements of hideous war in these fairy scenes?

We passed the night in the loveliest possible little harbour. Although we might almost have jumped ashore on either side, it took us some time to find water sufficiently shallow to anchor in. There were populous villages all around us, and we could see the people wandering to and fro, or collecting in chattering groups, after their day's toil. Then for a while, as evening closed, the fire-light gleamed through the paper windows of their neat cottages, and lanterns flitted past, looking like huge glow-worms in the distance; then darkness fell over all, and when the moon arose there was no motion and no sound in those busy little haunts; but there were watchers on board the *Berenice* who envied those sleepers their happy homes, and who, thinking of other homes far away, and of dear ones who they trusted also slept in peace, prayed God to guard them.

28*th October.*—Yesterday morning we saw the last of the Sowonada Seas, and skirted along the coast, which may boast its beauties too, though, I fear, our late feast has made us fastidious. To day we passed Hirado, the great coal depôt of Nagasaki, and, a few hours later, anchored, having reached the intermediate stage of our voyage.

I am afraid, after my late rhapsodies, to dwell upon the beauties around Nagasaki, the approaches and the bay of which are, perhaps, equal to the loveliest scenes in Japan, or in the world—but "their praise is hymned by loftier harps than mine." I have done for a while with landscape painting, and will only invite my

OUTSIDE SOWONADA.

readers' attention to my good friend Perreau's sketch of the Pappenberg, the last refuge and the scaffold of 20,000 Christians.

After having seen Yedo, Nagasaki offers little to surprise or interest the visitor. It is a rather dirty town, clinging uncomfortably to the side of a hill, and its streets are narrower, and its smells more offensive than, according to my experience, is usual in Japan. The principal shops are in the quarter called Decima; the prison in which Dutch merchants have been allowed to fatten and become rich, under laws and restrictions so humiliating that the contempt of the Japanese for a Hollander is not to be wondered at. The native wares exposed for sale, with the solitary exception of the egg-shell China, are very inferior to those of Niphon;* the bronzes are all modern, and the lacquer is mere rubbish. The people struck me as physically inferior; and they had, evidently, from more constant and longer intercourse with Europeans,

---

* The proper name of the central and principal island forming the Japanese groups. Niphon is said to signify "the source of the sun."

lost their very marked character, and appeared to
amalgamate more readily with foreigners than
those further north.

Unfortunately, the rainy season, which is,
I believe, a very long and frequently-recur-
ring one here, had set in; and I was unable,
during my short stay, to visit the environs
of Nagasaki, which, by all accounts, are very
beautiful.

The Russians appear to be quite at home here.
They had no less than four gunboats in the bay,
and had established a small naval colony on the
shore opposite to Nagasaki. In the remote
north in Yedo they have a firm foot-hold, and
if we do not keep a good look-out, some of these
days the big serpent will contract its folds and
hug the whole fair land in its merciful embrace;
not that there is any fear of Japan being con-
quered, but a judicious fomenting of the quarrels
and jealousies of rival or disaffected Daimios
might afford Russia the long-sought opportunity
of establishing an influence over these islands
under the term of a Protectorate, which would
prove as little beneficial to our interest in the

East as to the happiness or civilization of Japan.

For my own part, I am inclined to believe that a higher fate is in store for Japan, and that she is yet destined to play an important part in the future of Eastern empire, for she has within her, in spite of some serious blots, many of the elements of power and greatness.

Isolation from the rest of the world, while it has not deteriorated the physical condition, or checked the intellectual progress of the people, has strengthened their national virtues, courage, patriotism, love of order and country. Where is there another example of a race so entirely excluded from intercourse with others possessed of so high a degree of civilization? and, while obstinately clinging to their own ancient habits and traditions, so anxiously seizing, and bringing to bear upon their institutions, everything in art or science * calculated to advance them in

* When Count Eulenburg introduced the members of the Prussian Embassy, which he represented, to the Minister for Foreign Affairs in Yedo, that functionary appeared struck by the name of one of these. " Brandt! Brandt! Are you the author of a work on military tactics? " M. de Brandt re-

material prosperity, or to raise them in the scale of human intellect?

I do not pretend to say that a federal oligarchy* is the form of Government best calculated to develop the resources of the country or the prosperity of the people; but this has existed for ages (the present Siogoun or Tycoon is, I believe, the 127th sovereign of Japan), and will probably continue to exist, from time to time, more or less strengthened or weakened by innovations from without or internal struggles, until in the course of years and improvement the people shall feel their power, and demand a share in the government of the fair land for the masters of which they are now content to toil.

plied that his father had written such a work. " Oh," said the Minister, " it is very good; I had it translated from the Dutch into Japanese—I will give you a copy ; " and on the following day a Japanese translation of General de Brandt's " Treatise on the Three Arms " reached the Prussian Embassy. Is it a wonder that such a people manufacture rifled cannon, while the Chinese mount bamboo guns on their batteries?

* What else are we to call a Government partly feudal, partly monarchical, in which the majority of the nobles necessarily rule, and the nominal sovereigns are but the presidents of their Council?

But any such revolution to be safe must be gradual. The schemes of English and American enthusiasts to dethrone the Mikado and the Tycoon, dispossess the Daimios and introduce Constitutional Goverment or republican institutions, would simply result in converting a garden into a wilderness—an orderly and industrious people into a bloodthirsty mob—one of the finest countries in the world into a group of Russian coaling depôts and dock-yards.

Not that the conquest of Japan would be easy of accomplishment, although its dismemberment might. Foreign invasion would at once extinguish all internal feuds and jealousies, and unite the whole strength of the Empire against the common foe.

An attacking army would thus have to meet an entire nation, the great majority of which are trained from boyhood to the use of arms and habits of discipline.

To destroy their capital or their seaports, and to ravage their coasts would be easy, but to penetrate into the country, where alone a decisive blow could be struck; to maintain an

N

invading army in the midst of an injured, patriotic and courageous people; to carry cavalry or artillery through rice-fields and forests, over rivers and mountains, such as abound in Japan; and to overcome an enormous opposing force possessed of the great advantages of local knowledge—and though, of course, inferior in the science and practice of modern warfare, by no means ignorant of it, or devoid of organization and discipline—would be about the maddest and most fatal enterprise that an European general could possibly undertake. There is a vast difference between Japan and China.

Once more upon the waters. The line of coast grows dim; now it is but as a mist on the edge of the horizon—I have seen the last of fair Japan! *Vale!*

It is but a few months ago, and yet how dim and distant seem those fairy scenes!

Was I ever there? Did I really ride through the sweet green lanes of those remote islands in the Eastern seas? Did I in the flesh stand on the snowy peak of Fusi-jama, and from its height gaze upon the length and breadth of the fairest land in the world?

Did I actually, in the streets of that strange Yedo, meet the princely hawking-party, the quaint Daimio's procession, the swaggering band of two-sworded Yaconins, and the group of moosmes bathing at their doors?

Was I ever at Ojee, smoking drowsily under the shadow of camelias, and accepting of fragrant tea from a kneeling damsel—or did I dream it all?

Already my recollections of beautiful Japan fade into mist, like unsubstantial visions; and its scenes come back upon my memory, as does a familiar old tune, heard in days gone by, from a voice hushed for ever long ago!

PE-CHE-LI.

It is a great shock to the moral system, that plunge from the fair, green shores of Japan, to the swampy banks of the Peiho, of which I can just discern the outline, as we anchor in the midst of the fleet.

The sky is mud-coloured, the sea is mud-coloured, the land is mud-coloured, and, as our gun-boat approaches nearer, we can make out two mud-coloured forts, commanding the entrance of a mud-coloured river.

"That's where we landed last year," says a young Marine officer, as he points to an extensive mud-bank, intersected by ditches, and thickly planted with bamboo stakes, with their jagged points turned towards us; "there were about twenty of us got into that hole there, where you see that beam lying; and, by Jove! didn't they pepper us! only half-a-dozen got out of it."

He was a curly-headed, ruddy-cheeked boy, and looked as if he would, on the slightest provocation, go back into the same hole under the same circumstances.

" It must have been hot work," I suggest.

"I rather believe you; and wasn't the old Admiral cut up, neither? Wounds—oh, I don't mean that! *he* ain't the fellow to care for wounds, though it can't be pleasant to have a few inches of an iron cable driven into your side; but to have to sheer off before those d——d niggers—that's what hurt him!"

The poor lad had not a thought for the danger he had incurred, or the useless slaughter of his comrades : that was all in the way of their business, and they were paid for it; but a repulse, and by such an enemy, too, *that* rankled in his heart.

Any scheme more utterly hopeless than to effect a landing on that spot it would be difficult to conceive ; and when, in the course of the day, an officer at Taku led me to the Cavalier and round the batteries, I was at a loss whether most to wonder at the rashness and blindness of the men who planned, or the self-devotion and courage of those who attempted to execute, the first attack upon the Taku Forts.

My road lay to the north, and the prospect before me was not tempting to the eye, which could only take in an interminable mud-coloured plain, unrelieved by a tree, or a shrub, or a blade of grass, dotted here and there with mounds, graves, or huts (it was not easy to distinguish between them), among which meagre dogs prowled, with hungry eyes.

Only one other object glistens in the coppery glare of the setting sun. This is a high, white stone, marking the grave of an English officer. Had my friend or brother fallen here, I should have wrapped him in his cloak, carried him out to sea, and buried him in its blue depths, to save him from so desolate a sepulchre.

The distance, by land, between Taku and Tien-tsin is about twenty-eight miles (it is three times as long by the winding river route), over a broad and tolerably good road, as roads go in this charming country.

I engaged a native cart for my conveyance; a two-wheeled, covered vehicle, drawn by two mules, harnessed tandem-fashion; but, after a few miles' jolting, preferred taking my chance on foot. The smaller villages along the route were composed principally of tumble-down clay hovels, with a wretched, poverty-stricken population, but we passed several places of more pretentious character, and from the bustle in the streets, and the number of junks at the landing-places, having the appearance of trading ports of some importance; but, even here, there was an air of decay and squalor, which, perhaps, struck me the more forcibly from their contrast with the neatness and order of Japanese villages.

The people were not unfriendly, but stared at us as we passed with sullen indifference, showing as little disposition to molest as to assist us.

Night set in before I reached the straggling suburb of Tien-tsin, and here all was confusion in the narrow streets, the passage of which was frequently completely blocked up by broken-down carts and waggons.

The British soldier is certainly the least observant or communicative of men. I meet several, but not one can direct me on my way. He knows the number of his regiment, can probably tell you who commands his company, or even, if unusually smart, the name of his colonel; but I might as soon expect him to point out the position of an unseen star in the heavens, as to tell me the way to the Brigade-office or the Commissariat quarters, although he might be living next door to them.

Here comes a picquet, and I accost the sergeant in charge; but he only knows where his own barracks are, and " Don't know, sir," and " Can't say, sir," are his replies to all my inquiries.

" Why, surely you know where you draw your rations from ? "

" Yes, sir : Quartermaster's store."

" And where does the Quartermaster get them from ? "

" Don't know, sir."

" You don't know, sir? You don't mean to say that you don't know where the Commissariat is ? "

" Can't say, sir."

I remember hearing of an officer of a West
India regiment, in Jamaica, who, at an inspection of his corps—anxious to please a pious
general—made one of his men say grace after
dinner, and, by way of further proving the
spiritual progress made by the soldiers under his
command, asked,—

" To whom are you thankful for what you
have received ? "

The poor African looked puzzled.

" Whom do you thank for your daily bread,
my man ? "

" Commiss'ry offica ! " was the reply.

But the British soldier has no such gratitude
in his composition. He does not trouble himself to inquire whence his daily bread comes.

It was now quite dark, and, in wandering
about, I had evidently got out of the English
quarter of the town. I began to reflect
whether I had not better make myself comfortable for the night in my cart; but, on turning
to look, found that it had disappeared, with bag
and baggage. I then sat down on a doorstep,

and considered whether it might not be expedient to commit some offence for which I should be marched to the main guard, when a fat China-man, attended by a servant bearing a lantern, passes me. I give him to understand, with the eloquent gestures of despair, that I want to find my way to the military quarter of Tien-tsin. He at once understands me, and leads me, I am utterly at a loss to know by what instinct, to an extensive building, before which a sentry is pacing. I inquire of him—far from sanguine of getting a satisfactory reply—what post he is on? " Divisional Commissariat." So I say " Chin-chin " to my friend, with a deeply-grate-ful feeling and an intense admiration for his sagacity, and a few minutes afterwards find my-self among old friends, eating and drinking and talking of home and days gone by, till, fairly tired out, I borrow a sheepskin coat, in which I wrap myself, and sleep on the stone floor as soundly as ever I did in the most luxurious bed.

Tien-tsin, at this time, was not very unlike Balaklava in its worst days—as much confusion, dirt, hurry-skurry. Troops were pouring in, every hour, from Pekin (which had just been evacuated), and gun-boats were receiving them on board as fast as they arrived. At the same time, stores were being landed from the fleet for the force which was to winter in the north, and the landing-places were strewed with regimental baggage, fuel-wood, boxes of loot, forage, musical instruments, ammunition, bales of clothing, gun-carriages, horse-boxes, and bird-cages; among which officers and men floundered helplessly, in their attempts to reach their gun-boats or reclaim their property from the hands of the Coolie corps, who seemed to consider that, provided they worked, it mattered little whither they carried their burdens.

It was now the beginning of November, and the cold was already severe; towards the end of the month, the river began to freeze, and several gun-boats and other vessels on their way north, found themselves in permanent winter quarters, between Tien-tsin and Taku.

Unprovided with winter clothing, and living in houses with paper windows and stone floors,

and without fire-places,* we were not what may
be called comfortable; but the sufferings of the
poor Indian followers, principally Bengalese, who
had never even heard of such a thing as snow or
frost, were intense, and these were greatly aggra-
vated by their own improvidence and stupidity.
Before embarkation every man received certain
articles of warm clothing; but the temptation
was too strong for them: they gambled them
away or else packed them up carefully in the
hope of selling them to advantage; and, thinly
clad, bare-handed, bare-footed, they faced the
elements, and perished on the voyage, or returned
to their homes cripples from frost-bite.†

December had set in, with severity unusual in

* The Chinese rely principally upon their clothing to
keep out the cold. It is wonderful what a weight of fur
they can carry. Unlike ourselves, who undress to go to bed,
they put on additional clothing, and their morning toilette
in winter consists simply in putting on shoes, taking off a
robe or two, and untying their pigtails, which at night are
wound around the head.

† On board of a single junk, eighteen of these poor fellows
were frozen to death, between Tien-tsin and the anchorage in
the Gulf of Pecheli. Many of them had died in a state
of almost complete nudity, and their warm clothing was
found carefully stowed away in their kits.

these regions, before the last of the southward-bound left Tien-tsin; then the icy gates fairly closed upon us, and we had to make up our minds to be cut off for a few months from communication with the outward world, and to pass the winter of our discontent as best we might.

The force left to occupy the north of China and which, for some months to come, could, under no circumstances, hope for succour from without, was composed of three regiments of the line, one of irregular cavalry (Fane's Horse), and two batteries of artillery, with a proportion of Engineers, Military Train, Commissariat, and Medical Staff, under the command of Brigadier-General Staveley, who thought—and, I believe, thought justly—that with his little army he might march through the length and breadth of China, and defy anything that could be brought to oppose him.

Tien-tsin itself is simply a second-rate Chinese town, surrounded by a solid stone wall, about three miles in circumference, and in very bad repair, and by an outer mud wall and ditch, which embraces its extensive suburbs. This latter wall, which is fifteen miles in circumference, had been built since our attack on the Peiho Forts in 1859, but its merits as a defensive work were not tested when we marched upon Tien-tsin. A sandy plain stretches as far as the eye can reach in every direction around the city, and there is something inexpressibly dreary and desolate in that desert-like level, the dead monotony of which is increased rather than broken by the mud villages which at intervals of three or four miles dot its surface.

If the country around Tien-tsin has no beauty to boast of, the town offers even less attraction. Narrow streets, ingeniously contrived to accumulate mud and slush, traversed by open gutters and stagnant drains, in which the filth and refuse of the city fester and ferment; dirty, half-decayed houses, redolent of garlic, lamp-oil, and worse smells; naked beggars, exposing their hideous sores or deformities, and, now and then, a wretched woman, hobbling on the stumps of her feet,* and grimacing idiotically as she implores alms, with the eternal whining, "Chow-chowa, La-ya;" such are the principal objects which attract your notice in the good town of Tien-tsin; and here between three and four thousand Britons were thrown upon their resources for the means of getting through a long and severe winter.

It must be remembered that the army landed in the north in the very lightest marching order, and unfortunately the ice had set in before the arrival of the heavy baggage, so that our garrison was *sans* clothes, *sans* books, *sans* wines, *sans* everything; and dependent upon China tailors and furriers for warmth, upon Hong Kong and Shanghae shopkeepers (who charged 5*s.* for a black-lead pencil and 10*s.* for a tooth-brush) for their personal comforts, and, most hard of all,

* The horrible practice of cramping the feet, which prevails universally in the north, originated some 1200 years B.C., when the Emperor Cheu, to please a greater tyrant than even himself—his beautiful wife, Takya, who had, unfortunately, clubbed feet—issued an edict, that all women in the land should adopt the *chaussure* of the Empress. Can it be that any of our own absurdities in dress take their origin in the natural defect of some influential leader of fashion ?

upon their own heads for intellectual pursuits and mental recreation.

One of the first devices resorted to for killing time was (as is usual wherever British soldiers congregate) the formation of a theatrical company. A temple was quickly, and, thanks to the peculiar tastes of a young engineer officer, most artistically, converted into a regular theatre, with a practicable trap-door and a real green-room. The gallant commander of Fane's Horse—*beau sabreur* and *preux chevalier*, as accomplished as he is brave, and, if possible, more modest than either —became scene-painter and decorator. The Commissariat furnished a musical composer and director. The 60th Rifles contributed the orchestra, while every corps sent its representatives to strut their little hour upon the stage. Of course the company kept a poet and playwright, who, in the opening address, thus refers to the miseries and pleasures of a Tien-tsin existence :—

> " But, let me tell you, speaking of Tien-tsin,
> Worse places might be found than that we're in !
> Our quarters have their small defects, no doubt—
> Windows with draughts, and fire-place without ;

When tired of parade, or drill, or desk,
Our country rides are far from picturesque ;
Our news from home is scarce, and rather stale,
And females are still scarcer than the mail.*
But Mars, when banished from his usual haunts,
Still finds a substitute for all his wants.
Torn from beloved wife, or darling maid,
He seeks for solace in a piece of jade ;†
No Christmas-tree his festive feeling stirs,
So, 'stead of mistletoe, he takes to firs (furs?).
To bask in fair-skinned beauty no more able,
He learns to dote upon a skin of sable ;
And, freed from European fashion's trammels,
He rolls in silks, and revels in enamels ! "

" Loot," ‡ indeed, formed an inexhaustible subject of conversation and speculation ; its few fortunate possessors being never tired of

---

* This, and several other passages which I remember in the opening address, appear to be intended as a play upon the word, or what is commonly called a pun—a reprehensible description of humour in general, but rather popular in garrison towns.

† These and the following lines are in allusion to the " loot " taken om the Summer Palace.

‡ Loot, a Hindostanee word, signifying robbery or plunder, appears to have been regularly adopted in our language. The perpetrator of looting, who in India is called a " loot-wallah," or " robber," with us is frequently described as a hero. The French, whose army is full of heroes, and who never plunder, call looting " *biblotter!* "

expatiating upon the beauty and rarity of their wares, and the many less favoured, who had not seen the inside of Yuen-ming-Yuen, being ever ready to admire, to accept, or, at the worst, to purchase, some very curious or most extraordinary specimen of jade or enamel, as a *souvenir* of Pekin.

I may here mention that only a comparatively small number of officers or men had the opportunity of assisting at the sacking of the Summer Palace, or of sharing in the proceeds of its contents.   Sir Hope Grant had decided that prize-money should be received only by those who were actually present at the destruction of Yuen-ming-Yuen.   Thus, one regiment shivered on duty outside the walls and got nothing, while another, revelling in luxury within, was allowed to carry off all the booty.   I was not there at the time, or I should have been inclined to have submitted to the General's attention an authority on this subject, which he would have been the last man in the army to disregard.

In the First Book of Samuel, xxx. 24, it is written :—" As his part is that goeth down to the battle, so shall his be that tarrieth by the stuff: they shall share alike."

The value of the property in the Palace must have been enormous. The French are said to have had the pick of all; but they have been much misrepresented in this matter. It appears that the army lost its way, and, in searching for the appointed rendezvous, rambled by mistake into Yuen-ming-Yuen. Here the eunuchs, who acted as a guard, became so impressed by that politeness for which Frenchmen are distinguished, and which is particularly conspicuous among their soldiery, that they volunteered to show them all that was most curious and rare among the treasures under their charge, and even insisted upon their visitors accepting some of these as mementos. General Montauban, indeed, tells us himself that his army did not plunder, but only collected a few works of art, all of which were presented to the Emperor and Empress, with the exception of a few objects of interest reserved for national museums in France, and a *biblot* or two for the Princess Mathilde. The few trifles which the French officers and soldiers subsequently possessed, they had purchased from our men, who are terrible robbers.

Indeed, it was evident, when at length the French sentries allowed British officers to enter the Palace, that looting, in our sense of the word, had not been practised; for some colossal bronzes, a large collection of books and manuscripts, and even some jade and enamel ornaments, had remained untouched; and it was principally of such trifles as golden josses or ingots, or ewers, basins, and vases of the same metal, or pearls and other precious stones, curious for their size or brilliancy, or even of sycee silver (the solid wooden cases of which were considerately left behind) that our allies proved themselves connoisseurs and collectors.

The officers and men of our own army had been permitted to help themselves individually, but, on the day following, were required to deliver up their loot to the prize-agents, by whom it was sold for the common benefit of all present. This was a little hard, for while some officers had only lounged through the palace, and, having filled their pockets and their carts, went home to dine or sleep, others of more energy and greater powers of endurance made repeated trips, loading themselves, their soldiers or coolies, horses and waggons, again and again, and labouring like galley-slaves all the night through; yet these meritorious, hard-working men fared no better than their idlest comrades, or than the unaccountable prigs who voted looting an occupation derogatory to a British officer.

The amount of property which the allies removed, although considerable, was but small in comparison with that consumed by fire, on the palace * being destroyed; and even after this, it appears that a considerable quantity of valuables escaped both the rapacity of the flames and the plunderers.

It may be a matter of opinion whether the destruction of Yuen-ming-Yuen was a justifiable or a politic act; but that "looting" exercises an evil influence on the army cannot be ques-

---

* Yuen-ming-Yuen, be it remembered, is not a palace, according to our sense of the word, but an ornamental park, covering an area of four miles, with summer-houses, of greater or less extent, scattered throughout.

tioned. There is, perhaps, nothing more calculated to loosen the bonds of discipline, and to
damage the *morale* of a military body, than the
licence to plunder; and I fear I must add, that
it does not tend to improve the character of
British officers, but induces a mercenary spirit
not desirable, nor usually met with, among gentlemen in our army. *L'appétit vient en mangeant*,
and the taste of plunder in men, like the taste
of blood in wild beasts, begets in them an in-
satiable craving, difficult to control, and most
dangerous to gratify.

It was observed that troops who had served
in India were far more expert at looting than
others; they seemed to have reduced the business to a science, and they practised it like pro-
fessors.

Before the Battle of Sinho, the Celestial Go-
·vernment had fired the valour of their braves
by no less an indulgence than the issue of six
months' arrears of war-pay in hard silver. After
the action, it became speedily known among our
men, that each Chinaman had seven dollars on
his person, and a certain Queen's regiment was

particularly conspicuous for its powers of appropriation on this auspicious occasion. Nothing but long practice could have enabled men to acquire so methodical and business-like a way of ransacking the dead, the wounded, or the prisoners.

An ardent Hibernian distinguished himself above his fellows by the rapidity with which he secured and counted his spoils; but there was one dead Chinaman who seemed to puzzle him. He was seen to turn him over and over, evidently at a loss for something; searching now his pockets, now his boots, and diving into every nook of the dead man's clothes. It was in vain—there were only six pieces—one dollar was missing! Where could it be? One more search: it was no use, and time was precious, so Pat pocketed the sum, less the missing dollar; and, shaking his head sorrowfully at the corpse, exclaimed, in tones of melancholy reproach, "Ah, thin! ye profligate! you've been and spint one of them already!"

The frozen Peiho afforded some entertainment to our officers and men; and still more, perhaps, to the Chinese, who were inexpressibly delighted at our abortive efforts to learn their system of sledging. The sledge itself, upon which they convey heavy loads for very long distances, is simply a pair of runners connected by two cross-pieces, and covered with a piece of matting. The driver stands behind, with one foot on each runner, and, with an iron-shod pole which he places between his legs, propels his load along the ice at a marvellous pace, avoiding holes and fissures with as much nicety as an expert boatman steering his gig on a crowded river.

It requires long practice and a thick skull to acquire proficiency in this accomplishment, for a false move is pretty sure to send the driver flying backward on his head.

Coursing, with Chinese hounds, or occasionally with hawks trained for the purpose, races, steeple-chases, and cricket, completed the out-door exercises; but I must not omit to mention another occupation which helped to pass many a weary winter's day. This was curio-

، hunting in the shops of Tien-tsin, whither a very considerable quantity of unmistakable Yuen-ming-Yuen property had found its way, and was sold, while the mania in the garrison lasted, at prices more or less fabulous.

The Chinaman has an intense admiration for jade-stone, of which his seventh heaven is composed, while the sixth is only of gold. That most valued is of the purest and most delicate white, or of a peculiar shade of light green : in either, perfect transparency is indispensable to perfection, and the slightest flaw or blemish destroys the value.

Enamels on metal are likewise greatly prized. It is said that the secret of their manufacture has long since expired. I have seen some remarkably fine specimens of vases, but, as a rule, they are sadly devoid of form.

Good bronzes are extremely rare and not much appreciated.

But the great rage among Europeans in the north of China was for porcelain, of which there are so many varieties, each supposed to possess some peculiar charm or value, that the uninitiated are apt to give up the pursuit in despair. One kind, of a delicate yellow colour, with a green dragon emblazoned upon its surface, is only used by the Emperor; another, of a peculiar blue, is so rare that a broken cup is sold for five times its weight in gold. Yet both of these may be bought in Tien-tsin, and, in spite of their rarity, there is always a fresh specimen forthcoming as soon as the last "only one." has found a purchaser. I fear the curio-dealers formed a far higher opinion of our wealth than of our good sense: they must certainly have made small fortunes by us.

The picture-shops were an endless source of amusement: there you might see the English and French soldier in every imaginable dress, and in the most impossible attitudes; marching, fighting, marketing, and occasionally making love to a horrible creation of the artist's brain, supposed to be an European lady.

It is reported that no less a person than the wife of our Commander-in-chief was the first Englishwoman who sat, or rather walked, for her portrait to a Chinese artist, though I am rather inclined to suspect that he drew upon his imagination for everything but the hat, which is perfect, in all these drawings. I am confirmed in this view by the circumstance of no crinoline being introduced.

Our allies were, as a rule, represented in even a more ridiculous form than ourselves, and I believe, on more than one occasion, resented these caricatures rather seriously, as a national insult or a base reflection upon the glorious army of France; but our men were less susceptible, and heartily enjoyed the contemplation of red-coated monsters with their trousers buttoned behind, and carrying their firelocks with the left hand over the right shoulder.

The misery to be met with in the streets of Tien-tsin is harrowing. The thermometer has fallen to five degrees below zero, and yet hundreds of poor creatures, afflicted with all the ills that flesh is heir to—blind, lame, paralytic, idiotic, or lepered, lie huddled together on the stone pavements, chattering and shivering, or fighting as savagely as their little remaining strength will allow for any stray morsel of

food or small coin that may be flung among
them, till death, more merciful than man, puts
an end to their sufferings. Many a time did
the morning sun light upon the upturned face
of a corpse, lying unheeded among all that
breathing misery—unheeded! envied perhaps—
so placid, so calm, so happy, is its expression
in contrast with that of the living!

Want of charity is not among the faults of
the British soldier; many a time have I seen
our good fellows distributing, from their small
stores, food and money among these poor
wretches, while greasy, well-clothed Chinamen
would pass them without a look, or a thought
for their misery. Nor were efforts wanting in
the garrison to devise the means of affording
permanent relief to the poor.

A committee, headed by our chaplain, was
formed for this purpose, and a considerable
sum at once subscribed by officers and men;
whereupon the authorities were requested to
give notice that, on a certain day, a distribution
of alms would take place, and that a large attendance was requested. It was objected that

such a course would be attended with inconvenience, and attract all the poor or idle from miles around; but our committee was determined to be charitable in its own way, and the result was such a rush of applicants at the appointed time, that troops had to be ordered out to keep the ground, and no less than nine men, women, and children were killed, and twelve severely wounded, in the scramble for shilling-pieces. From this day, the number of beggars in Tien-tsin increased tenfold.

A more judicious measure was set on foot by Dr. Lamprey, an army surgeon, who established a Chinese Hospital, and devoted himself, with most praiseworthy zeal, to alleviating the misery of the poor wretches, who eagerly sought his aid. The means at his disposal were necessarily limited, but he had the satisfaction of being enabled to afford relief to thousands of sufferers, and of restoring to a large number the blessing of sight, to which they had long been strangers.*

* Neglected ophthalmia, with want of cleanliness, is one of the principal causes of the blindness which prevails so greatly among the poor in China.

The fortitude of the Chinese, under the most severe operations, was the wonder of all. Not only men, but women and children would submit themselves to the knife without flinching, and undergo even the amputation of a limb without a cry or complaint.

There is a theory that the sense of pain is possessed in proportion to the sense of enjoyment; perhaps this may account for the stoical endurance of the poor Chinese, whose experiences of pleasure in this life are certainly few in comparison with their many sufferings.

From my Diary.—January 18.—Attended the funeral of General Collineau, Commander-in-chief of the French Army in the north of China, who died from the effects of confluent smallpox, on the 15th.

He had seen much service, and was considered a good general. His last words were expressions of regret at having, after getting through fifteen general actions, to die at last in his bed at Tien-tsin.

The French funeral ceremonies differ widely from those of our army, but are not less impressive. The band of the 102nd Regiment played Verdi's "*Miserere*" with admirable taste in the chapel. During the procession to the burial-ground, there was no music but the Zouaves' "Quick Step" (the general had commanded a regiment of Zouaves in the Crimea, and led them in the storming-party at the Malakoff); and their *reveillé* were the last notes over his grave.

Service was performed on this occasion by three missionary bishops; two of them Frenchmen, one a Chinaman, but all wearing the Chinese dress, pigtail included. The effect was novel if not imposing.

The addresses spoken over the grave were short, pithy, and soldier-like; that of the army chaplain concluded thus :—

"*Messieurs, je n'ai plus rien a vous dire;*" then, with a wave of his hat towards the open grave, "*Adieu, mon Général, au revoir!*"

Tien-tsin is full of temples, and the people much prefer their being handed over as barracks and quarters for our forces to letting their own private houses.

A Chinaman lives with all his belongings about him. An Englishman, and sometimes even an Englishwoman, thinks it a hard case to have a mother-in-law quartered upon him or her; what would they say to having three or four generations, from grand-parents down to third cousins-in-law, and each with his or her immediate belongings, living under one roof and dining at one common table? To the poor this arrangement must be somewhat inconvenient, but the residences of the wealthier classes consist of a number of detached dwellings within one enclosure, forming, as it were, a small colony, where all, under the presidency of the head of the house, live as much like the "happy family" at Waterloo Bridge as is possible under the circumstances. These residences are convertible into capital officers' quarters and barracks for a small number of troops, but are, unfortunately, constructed with little regard to either the

STABLES OF FANE'S HORSE

means of warmth or of ventilation. The ornamental is, however, never neglected; the oak
carving of doors, window-frames, arches, &c., is
admirable; and by the introduction of glass,
fire-places, and stoves, and, in summer, of sun-
shades and punkahs, we managed to make ourselves tolerably comfortable. When troops occupied temples, they were enjoined, by notices
placarded on the walls, not to "meddle with
the gods," and, beyond sticking pipes into their
mouths, decorating them with moustaches, or
turning their extremities into clothes-pegs, the
British soldier was rarely guilty of sacrilege.

It took the officers of the 31st Regiment
some time to get accustomed to the presence of
a number of gigantic josses which were ranged
along one side of their mess-room, glared at
them at their meals, and savagely witnessed
their orgies.

The stables of "Fane's Horse" were, in like
manner, presided over by gods so hideous that
any horse of an excitable temperament, who
should wake up suddenly in the night, would
have been quite justified in going into fits at the

P

sight of them, as they sat there glowering by the dim lamplight.

The French, who exclusively occupied the right bank of the Peiho, while our troops were quartered on the left, treated the *habitans* with less ceremony than we showed them. Their system was, to *order* whatever buildings they required for their troops; indeed, all their wants were supplied, in the same manner, upon a *requisition*, which the authorities did not run-the risk of failing to comply with, and for which they rarely expected and still more rarely received payment; whereas we, who paid handsomely for everything, were served with far less alacrity, and were, upon the whole, decidedly less popular. It was curious to notice how the French soldier fraternized with the Chinaman, and how quickly and perfectly they managed to make themselves mutually understood. Even on our side of the water, the words " *Dit, donc,*" and " *Combien?* " were long in force before they were superseded by the Anglicized version of " I say," and "Owmush?" What the market-people and shopkeepers meant by their constant cry of " fish " I was never able to make out. It was odd enough to see them holding up an enamel vase or a fur robe, or a basket of eggs, or a brace of birds, for your inspection, and exclaiming, " I say—fish ! fish !—how mush ? "

It was literally all fish that came to their net.

The British soldier made no progress in the Chinese tongue, but was very impatient of similar incapacity on the part of a " Chinee " or " Fokee," as he calls the natives. The following conversation occurred under my window the other evening :—

Officer's Servant (loquitur).—Now, look you here, Fokee ! There's no use your talking to me. I won't have it. I don't understand your d——d lingo, so shut up ; but just you listen to me. If you don't be here by daylight to-morrow, and have that 'ere fire lighted, and this 'ere biler filled by the time I get up, I'll give you such a hiding as you've never had yet ; so, now, wilo,* Fokee, and mind what I tell you."

* " To wilo, *v. a.* to be off ; to disappear.—*Vulg.* to mizzle." —*Dictionary of Pidjen-English.*

Fokee nods his head, with a grin, and " wilos " accordingly, not without a certain instinctive knowledge of what is expected of him; while the Briton says to his comrade,—

" They are a poor ignorant lot, them Fokees, aint they, Bill?" whereunto Bill responds with an assenting sigh of pity and a proud sense of intellectual superiority.

The necessity of making certain arrangements connected with a military detachment about to be quartered at Pekin, as a guard and escort for the British Legation, afforded me an opportunity of paying a visit to the capital, which, for no better reason than that it has long been inaccessible, always excites the interest and curiosity of Europeans.

At this time Mr. Bruce, our Envoy in China, had not yet taken up his residence in Pekin, where Mr. Wade, then his Chinese secretary, had gone, some months previously, as *avant courier*, to prepare the Chinese mind for the presence of British diplomatists, and perhaps at the same time to re-assure British diplomatists as to the disposition of the Chinese mind.

If Mr. Wade had had his throat cut or been burnt in his house during the winter, his chief would probably have discovered that the treaty might have been enforced and our commerce extended through the less dignified medium of a consul, and without the presence of a minister plenipotentiary and envoy extraordinary.

Accompanied by Mr. Dick, an excellent Chinese scholar, attached as interpreter to the Commissariat, I left Tien-tsin on the 18th of March, and, after a three days' ride through as uninteresting a country as can well be conceived, came in sight of the fine solid wall which encloses the straggling mass of ruin, dirt, and decay, called Pekin.

Chinese villages are, at best, dreary and squalid-looking, but on this route, where the dogs of war have so recently been let loose, there is something harrowing in the misery and desolation of the scene. Has grinding oppression and long suffering deadened the heart of the Chinese peasant to all sense of injury? Or has he, after all, a Christian feeling of forgiveness towards his enemies, for which no orthodox Church-man would give the Pagan credit? I cannot explain it, but I own to something like a sense of shame having come over me as we two solitary unarmed strangers passed through crowds of men, women, children, standing by the charred ruins of their homesteads and among their shattered household gods, without being met by a single angry look or gesture—nay, more, always re-ceiving a ready and friendly reply to every ques-tion. Perhaps, they felt grateful that we had, at any rate, spared their wretched lives, which is more than they can expect from their country-men, the Taypings, when they pay them a visit.

Some of the villages along our road were mere heaps of rubbish; others retained more or less the semblance of human habitations. In the larger ones, such as Ho-si-woo, which it may be remembered was for some time in occupa-tion of our troops, the late enemy's inscriptions on doors and walls seem to be piously preserved as agreeable relics, and such familiar garrison words as "Officers' Quarters," "Canteen,"

"Fane's Horse," "Commissariat," "General Hospital," &c., meet one at every turn; though one cannot but remark with regret, that the buildings which appear to have afforded shelter to the invaders, are sadly devoid of everything in the shape of woodwork, which was probably used, as occasion required, for cooking dinners and boiling water. A celebrated and imposing pawnbroker's shop which was "looted" here, has not yet recovered itself; but let it be borne in mind, that in pillage, as in wanton destruction, the Chinese themselves far excel the British, or even the French, soldier. The bonds of restraint once removed, and a Celestial mob have no patriotic, religious, or humane scruples as to the property of mandarin, priest, or peasant—as they fully exemplified at the sacking of Yuen-ming-Yuen and the Llama Temple, the sacred proceeds of which are to this day openly offered for sale in the shops of Tien-tsin, and even, under the very eyes of the authorities, in Pekin.

At Ho-si-woo, we met a French missionary bishop on his way to Europe, after having passed twenty-five years in China. He was dressed in

complete native costume, and appeared to be
treated with great reverence by the unbelieving
crowd who flocked in to see the "mandarin
priest." The self-devotion, the zeal, and, as a
very general rule, the pure and simple lives led
by the French missionaries in China (and their
number throughout the empire and the kingdom
of Siam exceeds 1500), are not without their
effect upon the people, although this is not indicated by wholesale and indiscriminate conversion
to nominal Christianity.

Passing over the fine stone bridge of Palichou,
which bears unmistakable marks of the French
cannon, and where a craven mandarin, smart-
ing from a wound, ordered poor Brabazon to
be decapitated, we came upon the broad paved
road leading into Pekin. This was in such
wretched repair, that we preferred a path running parallel with it, and which, after a weary
dusty ride of three or four hours, brought us to
the Chan-yung gate of the Celestial capital.
Another three miles through wide streets flanked
by trees, and resembling rather the suburb of a
provincial town than the interior of the most

populous city in the world, led us to the portal of Liang-kung-fu, the residence assigned to the British Legation—a straggling, dreary, dilapidated building, which time and money might convert into a tolerably-habitable barrack for a brigade of infantry, but which can never become a comfortable or suitable residence for a Minister and the few members of his suite.*

Europeans are still novelties in Pekin. A few grandees whom we met in chairs, and some mandarins, numerously attended, on horseback, carefully averted their gaze from the offensive foreign devils as we passed; but the shopkeepers came to their doors, and stared at us with mild curiosity, and the mob, and more particularly its juvenile portion, followed us in crowds, and occasionally saluted us with expressions more familiar than polite. Upon the whole, however, we had no reason to complain of the conduct of the people; the race of *gamins* is much the same all the world over.

* I understand that time and money, backed by good taste, have done more than I gave them credit for, and that the Legation is both handsomely and comfortably fitted up.

A three days' ramble through Pekin, or, at least, those parts accessible to foreigners (against whom the official quarter is hermetically closed), shewed me little to admire, if I except the Wall and one lovely view, called Pay-hay, formed of a picturesque group of temples, embosomed in trees, on the borders of an ornamental piece of water. Dirt, ruin, and bad smells reign supreme in the capital of the "Lord of Ten Thousand Years."

On expressing my intention of visiting the Great Wall, the nearest part of which is about 50 miles from Pekin, in an almost due northerly direction, I was, of course, told of the many insuperable obstacles to be overcome, the risk of falling into the hands of the rebels, of being attacked by robbers, and, more perilous than all, of meeting the Emperor on his entry into the capital; but old travellers in the East are accustomed to these auguries, and I started, together with Mr. Dick, confident that bad roads and rough fare would prove our worst enemies. Passing out of the Antin Gate (through which our army made its entry), we

made a *détour* of a mile or two to visit the
Russian cemetery, where a hideous stone monument, bearing the following inscription, has
been erected to the memory of our poor murdered countrymen :—

Sacred
TO THE MEMORY OF
CAPTAIN L. B. BRABAZON, R.A. ;
LIEUTENANT R. B. ANDERSON, FANE'S HORSE ;
PRIVATE S. PHIBBS, 1ST DRAGOON GUARDS ;
W. DE NORMAN, ESQUIRE, ATTACHÉ TO HER MAJESTY'S LEGATION ;
T. H. BOWLBY, ESQUIRE ; AND
EIGHT SIKH SOLDIERS ;
WHO,
TREACHEROUSLY SEIZED,
IN VIOLATION OF A FLAG OF TRUCE,
ON SEPTEMBER 10, 1861,
SUNK UNDER THE INHUMAN TREATMENT
TO WHICH THEY WERE SUBJECTED
BY THE CHINESE GOVERNMENT
DURING THEIR CAPTIVITY.

What Englishman can stand before that stone
and think of the terrible tortures inflicted upon
those brave men, to most of whom death so
slowly brought relief, without feeling that the
most treacherous and foul murders ever committed under the sanction of a Government
have been but inadequately avenged ? and that

the destruction of a miserable tyrant's palace, and the exaction of a few thousand pounds, are but poor compensation for such lives as have been lost to the country. That the authors and perpetrators of outrages, the full extent of which has never yet been divulged, are known, and might have been brought to justice, admits of no doubt. The cowardly murderer of poor Brabazon lives, and holds, to this day, a high command under his Imperial master. Not one of all who instigated or executed tortures and death upon their helpless victims has been brought to justice, although to have hanged such wretches from the highest turret of the walls of Pekin would have done more towards teaching the Chinese Government humanity than all the verbose diplomatic notes or edifying sermons that could be written or preached.

An old Chinaman, a devout Christian (if crossing one's self frequently be proof of faith), is the guardian of the cemetery. He pointed out the order in which the bodies of Anderson, De Norman, Bowlby, and Phibbs lie buried (that of Brabazon has not been traced yet);

but there is nothing to distinguish the different graves, or, indeed, to show that human remains lie beneath the sandy soil upon which you stand.*

Passing the Llama Temple, which an inscription in chalk tells us served as Military Train stables during the occupation, and which bears terrible marks of the spoiler's hand, we proceeded on our route through a sterile tract of country, and, reaching the village of Hareilung-koun at night, slept at a small inn, in company with some twenty or thirty cut-throat-looking Mongolian soldiers on their way to fight the rebels.

---

* Since this was written, I learn that Mr. Bruce has caused mounds to be erected over the different graves. The father of Major Brabazon, naturally enough, not satisfied with the measures taken by the authorities for seeking proofs of his son's death, visited Pekin in September, 1861, but, in spite of large rewards offered by him, could obtain no reliable information. Our diplomatists assured him that the surest way not to learn anything from Chinamen was to ask them questions, but they failed to suggest what the proper method was for getting at the truth. I fear it cannot be denied that reprehensible apathy was shown in this matter.

Another day's journey brought us to Chataou—
a hamlet at the foot of the Great Wall. The road
for the last fifteen miles had been so bad that
we were obliged to leave our horses at Nankau,
hiring in their place Tartar ponies. Nothing
less surefooted than these shaggy, hardy, little
beasts could have carried us through the
rugged mountain paths, which we would have
traversed on foot but that one mile's march over
the sharp rock which forms the pavement would
have left us shoeless.

At daybreak on the following morning we
climbed the highest peak of the mountain range,
and there, standing on the top of the Great
Wall, reflected upon the stupendous folly of this
wonderful work of human industry, which is
said to have cost the country 200,000 lives
from sheer physical exhaustion. The Wall,
which is built of stone and brick, is here twenty
feet high and fifteen feet broad, surmounted by a
double parapet, loopholed towards the north. As
far as the eye can follow the mountain range it
winds over the ridges of the precipitous black
rocks, like a gigantic serpent crawling along, and

with its breath poisoning all around; for, turn where you will, nothing meets the view but the desolate, dreary tract of rock, unrelieved by a blade of grass or a tuft of moss, and huge boulders strewing the base of the mountain sides. It was the whim of a tyrant to construct an artificial wall where Nature had already built a barrier far more effectual than anything that human art could create. However, there it remains, after a lapse of nearly 2000 years—a monument of the cruel folly of one man, and the patient industry and sufferings of millions.

Having made an abortive attempt at a sketch, and tried in vain to discover one redeeming future in this vast scene of desolation, I secured a brick as a memento, and, descending to the pass, proceeded homewards. Our guide could hardly believe his senses—certainly he doubted ours. When at Nankau, mine host inquired what we were going to the Great Wall for, our honest answer met with no credit. Were there no walls elsewhere? Was not the Wall of Pekin much better worth looking at? And then, as for shooting, why come so far for game when it could be bought in the market, at our very doors? His impression evidently was that we had some sinister project in view; but when we returned with the brick the good man simply burst out laughing, and probably set us down for a couple of harmless idiots.

Before entering Pekin, I paid a visit to the Summer Palace, and, meeting with no obstruction, found my way through the outer enclosure into the midst of the ruins of Yuen-ming-Yuen. The work of destruction seems, after all, to have been tolerably complete, and not the least effort has been made to restore grounds or buildings; shells of grotesque houses and pagodas, heaps of ruins and cinders, charred beams, and trees with their drooping branches singed to death, meet you at every turn, though I did here and there discover a building that appeared to have escaped detection, or, perhaps, was gutted without having been afterwards fired. At one of the principal gates, two monstrous bronze lions, valued at £5000 each, remain intact upon their massive pedestals. Certainly it would have required the greater part of the transport of the army to carry them away. I suppose I ought to have felt indignant at seeing the ruin we have made of a very fair scene, but the poor harmless villager, whose wretched hut was burnt over his head, had exhausted all my sympathies. I thought of the graves in the Russian cemetery, and felt almost disposed to regret that the Emperor and his courtiers had not been included in the conflagration.

Pursuing my researches, I was stopped at one of the inner gates by some eunuchs, forming the Palace-guard, and while parleying with them, a mandarin, numerously attended, emerged from the interior, and requested us to retire, as our remaining or penetrating further would be attended with serious consequences to himself. He was perfectly polite and so was I, and, of course, I obeyed orders, and rode away.

On approaching the British Legation, I saw the tricolor flying over an adjoining wall, the French Minister having on that day made his entry. Mr. Bruce arrived on the following morning.

In spite of the advice of an accomplished and

Q

experienced member of his Legation, who has been a little too long in China, and who feared that the sight of the English colours might wound the susceptible feelings of the poor dear Chinese officials, the Union Jack now flies in Pekin.

It is surely time that our diplomatists should have learnt that in dealing with the most false and corrupt Government in the world they have more to gain by a manly and independent attitude than by truckling to prejudices or submitting to insolent pretensions.

We had been so long accustomed to hear that Mr. Bruce relied entirely upon his own influence and the good faith of the Chinese for maintaining his position, and not at all upon a military force, which was rather an obstacle than an aid to his success, that the garrison of Tien-tsin was a little surprised, and a great deal disappointed, when, towards the end of April, Admiral Hope, on his return from Pekin, announced that the result of his conference with the Minister was a determination that the Army of Occupation should not be removed or reduced for the present; and that we might make up our minds to a summer in Tien-tsin, and, in all probability, for a winter, too.

This was a damper to most of us, who had indulged in hopes of an early return to England— to join our families, or to attend the Derby, or to be in time for strawberries and cream, or to see Blondin, or to hear Spurgeon, or to get married, according to our tastes, dispositions, or circumstances; but there was no help for it, and so we set to work and demolished fireplaces and partitions, and constructed windows and punkahs, and organized races and steeple-chases, and established a billiard-room and bowling-alley, and got up boats' crews for our gigs, and ordered mess stores from Shanghae or Hong Kong, and, in a word, determined to make the best of a melancholy state of things, as Her Majesty's liege subjects serving in her army so often have to do.

The shopkeepers have been waiting to learn our fate before they replenish their stocks, and now they send off orders for a large supply of South African port and sherry (a great bargain —only twenty dollars a dozen !) ; of gooseberry wine, to be labelled "champagne," and sold at only 10*s.* a bottle; of spirits of wine, diluted and mixed with brown sugar, labelled " *Vieux Cognac* " ; of boots and shoes, and ready-made summer clothes, and fancy perfumery, and volumes of the "Railway Library"; of cricket-bats and balls, and Hunt's playing-cards, and many other things, all of a curiously bad quality, and procurable at an advance of only two or three hundred per cent. on cost prices.

Prices rise gradually in China, as you travel north. In Hong Kong an English shilling's-worth costs you a dollar; in Shanghae, a tael (6*s.* 8*d.*) ; and in Tien-tsin about ten shillings, without reference to vulgar fractions.

But, after all, what right have we to complain? Why do we lead such artificial lives, and within a few miles of Pekin require all the luxuries of London?—English beer, and French and Spanish wines; sauces and *pâtés* from

Fortnum and Mason, and soda-water from Schweppe?

The markets of Tien-tsin are wonderfully well supplied. There you have fish, meat, game, vegetables, and fruits in the greatest profusion,. and at the lowest prices. There is a Celestial Gunter, whose confectionary and sweetmeats are unrivalled in their way; and our cooks might take some useful lessons from their Chinese fellow-craftsmen.

They manage these things better across the river. Our allies save their money for better times, instead of lavishing it on bad European luxuries; they subsist entirely upon local resources, eat native chow-chow, employ native tailors and booters, drink samshoo as a liqueur, acquire the use of chopsticks, and turn up their noses at sponges and clean linen.

We Englishmen are abject slaves to habit, and if we will insist, even in China, on having capers with our boiled mutton, and upon washing our flannels and persons, why we must pay for it, that is all!

Count Eulenburg, the Prussian Ambassador, arrived here in the beginning of May. I had met him, and the gentlemen attached to the embassy, in Japan, where he had successfully concluded an international treaty. He had now come on a similar mission to China, and although receiving no support or assistance from the representatives of the established treaty Powers, and opposed by a strong influence in Pekin, he accomplished his object in the course of a few months.

There is, after all, and in spite of Captain Macdonald and the magistrates of Bonn, a strong affinity and natural alliance between us and the Prussians. Of course, we look down upon them and see in their ways a great deal to condemn and ridicule : they are only foreigners ! But, making allowance on this score, they approach more nearly to our ideas of perfection— that is to say, to Englishmen—than any nation we know of.

Count Eulenburg and almost all the members of the embassy spoke English fluently. They could discuss our politics, institutions, and sports

without falling into the ludicrous blunders
which the most Anglicized Frenchmen invariably
commit: they never offered their guests bottled
porter with their desert; they went out shooting
in thick-soled shoes and without embroidered
game-bags; and not only joined in all our sports,
but gave us a handsome cup to be run for at our
races. In a word, they proved a great acquisition to the society of Tien-tsin, and even young
subalterns would admit, with a patronizing air,
that "those Prussians ain't half bad fellows!"
Yet people say that Englishmen are prejudiced
against foreigners!

As one who has run the gauntlet of our worst
stations all over the globe, and been accustomed
to the extremes of heat and cold to which in
our tour of colonial service we are exposed, I
will venture to place Tien-tsin at the very head
of the worst summer climates. There may be
greater heat, though I have never experienced it
—112° in the shade is well enough—but for a
thorough-going sleep-destroying, liver-corroding,
spirit-lowering, knock-me-down kind of temperature, this ranks before the worst stations of the

East and West Indies, and, by all accounts, takes
the *pas* even of the swamps on the Western
Coast of Africa.

Extraordinary precautions had been taken to
prevent the troops from exposing themselves
out of doors during the day, but the sun pursued its victims into the shade, and our poor
men became subjected to its malignant influence
under the form of what the doctors called " heat
apoplexy," by which they were attacked in their
barrack-rooms and even in their beds, and from
which recovery was rare.

It was with grateful feelings that, during the
most trying period of the summer, I accepted an
invitation from Commodore Sundewall, commanding the Prussian Squadron which had accompanied the Embassy, to pass a week or two
on board the *Arcona*, a fine steam-frigate, lying
in the Gulf of Pecheli.

The Commodore, a Swede by birth, had served
some years in our navy, spoke our language like
a native, and was in his manner and appearance
the *beau ideal* of a British sailor. Most of the
officers spoke English fluently, and but for their

hideous caps—similar to those worn in the Russian service—and the Frederick-the-Great cut of their marines, one was apt to fancy himself on board an English man-of-war.

They appear to have adopted all our words of command and technical terms, and it was curious to hear our naval phraseology rendered, as "Shoven sie off," "Bring mir das logbuch," "Pullen sie weg," &c.

The good Commodore was all courtesy and kindness; his officers were high-bred and accomplished men, and, probably from the nature of their career, less stiff-necked and opinionated than Prussians generally are; the men were sturdy, ruddy-cheeked, active fellows, and there was a general air throughout the ship of smartness, cleanliness, and regularity, which we are apt to believe peculiar to our own service.

We had a delightful week's cruise among the Miau-tow Islands, anchoring frequently, and landing to walk, explore, shoot, or bathe. There was here a very sensible difference of temperature, and the scenery was extremely pretty; though, probably, I had so long been accus-

tomed to the monotonous ugliness of Tien-tsin
that I exaggerated its beauties. During our
trip we passed within sight of Ning Hai,
where the Great Wall terminates in a pagoda by
the sea-shore. Otherwise there was little noteworthy. It was curious, however, to observe
how the poor people inhabiting these islands—
some of which are little more than rocks, of
volcanic formation—managed to coax some kind
of nourishment out of the barren soil; for
wherever a blade of grass could be got to grow,
there we found vegetation. Yet, even here,
where hard and continuous labour could barely
produce the means of maintaining a wretched
existence, the official grip was on the poor
peasant; and the meagre patch of rice, or
maize, or the string of bony fish, or the stock
of coarse grass, painfully gathered among the
rocks for the coming winter's fuel, had to yield
their tax to the lazy official, whose greedy eye
nothing can escape—for whose greedy appetite
nothing is too gross, too great, or too mean.

Truly, they are a patient, industrious, long-
suffering race, those many millions of poor

Chinese peasants, who, generation after generation, are content to be hewers of wood and carriers of water—hungering, perishing, fainting, but toiling on painfully, from sunrise to sunset, to contribute to the maintenance of some filthy mandarin! Can we wonder that they hold life cheap? that to them death has no sting, and the grave no victory? that the wretch sentenced to die by the hands of the hangman, can, for a few shillings, purchase a substitute, and prolong his own miserable existence at the price of a life yet less valued or worthless than his own?*

I was once assured by a French missionary,

---

* It is beyond a doubt that the practice of criminals, under sentence of death, being allowed to provide a substitute, prevails very generally. A son will occasionally, out of filial affection, offer his head in place of his father's. Old men past work, or old women past bearing, will, in like manner, redeem the life of a younger and stronger member for the benefit of their families; but some money payment is always exacted by the officials before they ratify these bargains. In Canton it became so common for old people to place themselves in their canoes under the bows of a steamer, to enable their relatives to claim compensation for their deaths, that our shipowners were obliged to come to the determination to entertain no claims for damages on account of drowned Chinamen.

who had passed the greater part of his life in the interior of the country, that the laws of China are framed in a spirit of equity and justice, if not of mercy; that although their administration was corrupt, venal, and tyrannical, gross acts of oppression or cruelty were checked, not only by the fear of detection and punishment from superior authority, but by a kind of public opinion which the masses can bring to bear upon their rulers; that life and property were, as a rule, well protected, and the exactions of Government officials, although oppressive, yet kept within recognized bounds; above all, that the right of petition was held sacred, and that the highest official would patiently hear, and generally promptly redress, the grievances of the poor.

It is very difficult to reconcile such views with what common observation and experience teaches an European; with the open and insolent corruption of the officials one meets, with their undisguised dishonesty, fraud, and greed, and their vile lives;* with the slavish submission, the un-

---

* Gross as is the immorality of the Japanese, these are a virtuous race in comparison with the Chinese, more particularly those of the north, where unheard-of profligacy is

complaining misery, and the squalor of the mass of the people; with the barbarous punishments which prevail, and the wholesale butcheries committed in the name of the law; with the significant fact that those who have gained anything, no matter by how much honest industry or thrift, hoard and hide it to escape confiscation of their property, and that one hundred thousand heads may fall by the hand of the executioner in the course of a single year without creating surprise or remonstrance.

Can such things be under a Government professing even a semblance of justice and humanity? The ruffian Yeh is reported to have executed no less than 70,000 men during the term of his vice-royalty; and the cruelties commonly committed upon offenders at Canton, while our troops occupied the city, were so outrageous, that the English general, upon his own authority, interfered to put a stop to them, or, at any rate, to their perpetration in public.

not only tolerated, but licensed by the Government. It is impossible to dwell upon so repulsive a subject, but if ever a land has, by its vices, merited the blighting curse of the Almighty, that land is China.

One can hardly traverse a street in a Chinese
town without meeting with poor creatures
blinded, lamed, hamstrung, or otherwise mutilated by the hand of the torturer. An English
officer who attended the trial of some Chinamen
charged with a violent assault on one of our
soldiers at Pekin, gave a graphic description of
how, at a given signal from the judge, a number
of torturers—hideous, maimed wretches who had
bought their forfeited lives by adopting this trade
—sprang like so many enraged demons upon
their prey, and dragged them, amid ribald jests
and triumphant imprecations, to their dens,
there to inflict all that the refinement of cruelty
could conceive or poor humanity bear.

I was once shown a book containing an account of the tortures authorized by law, but was
assured that, with the view of extorting money,
or to vent private enmities, the officials far exceeded these limits.

The names of some of the legalized tortures
indicate a certain ghastly humour or playfulness
on the part of their inventors or executioners.
One is called " The Frame of the Flowery Eye-

brow," another " The Monkey Sucking a Peach,"
a third " The Affectionate Snake," a fourth
" The Bridal Bed," and so on.

Lest the poor victim should, by any effort of
his own, accelerate death to escape agony, he is
assured that these earthly torments are but a
slight foretaste of those to come hereafter.

In every Chinese town there is, at least, one
" Temple of Horrors," in which there are large
figures, carved in wood, representing the condition of the wicked in a future state. The
minuteness of detail, the richness of fancy, the
inventive genius of the implacable tormentors,
and the hopeless despairing agony of the victims,
are depicted with such perfection, that the contemplation of a Chinese Inferno leaves a truly
pious Christian nothing to wish for as regards
the fate of his sinful fellow-creatures. The only
error, which, let us hope, the zeal of our missionaries will dispel, is that the worst punishments have a term. The Chinese mind cannot,
in its heathen ignorance, grasp the idea of an
eternity of suffering.

Governed and educated as they are, can we

wonder that the Chinese are a cruel race?—that parents look on with pride and satisfaction, while their little ones amuse themselves by dismembering an insect, or plucking a bird alive?—that a cook cannot kill a fowl without first torturing it?—and that no spectacle so much delights a Chinese mob as the flogging,* mutilation, or execution of one of their fellows? Not one among that grinning crowd but feels that it may be his turn next; and when it comes, he bears his fate with the stoical firmness or the stolid indifference peculiar to heroes and slaves.

Divine service is performed in Tien-tsin in the Hall of Kung-fu-tse (or, as we call the great philosopher and moralist, *Confucius*), where competitive examinations are also held for admission to various public offices.

We all know that the competitive system, which we have lately introduced into England,

* The punishment commonly inflicted in Tien-tsin for trifling offences consists in beating the culprit *on the face* with bamboos, until all trace of features is obliterated.

originated, many centuries ago, in China, where it produced admirable fruits; indeed, the high morality of their public men is mainly attributable to this institution.

The subject may be uninteresting to my general readers, and, if so, they will skip the next few pages; but it may prove instructive to the advocates of competitive examination, as a test of fitness for public office, and to the Civil Service Commissioners, to learn how their favourite system is worked in China; and I consider myself fortunate in having been able to obtain (through a peculiar source inaccessible to any other European) an examination paper of the last successful candidate at Tien-tsin.

This young gentleman, whose name is Sia-Lau, was one of 1223 competitors for the office of Ninth Acting Assistant to the Chief Clerk of the Sub-Director of the Scavenging Branch of the Military Board of Works.

In order to test his capacity for this responsible post, he was only required, in common with his 1222 fellow-candidates, to prove his perfect proficiency in navigation, hydrostatics,

the elements of the theological system introduced by Hang-eu, in the reign of Ping-te, with
the leading features of the dogmas subsequently
propagated by Bung-ho, under Ho-te. Further,
he was expected to have a sound knowledge of
astronomy, of the light literature most popular
in the year 2, of the principles of gunnery,
anatomy, and mensuration, and of the secret
history of the eunuchs at the Court of Pekin
from the beginning of the world, down to the
accession of Hien Fung.* Lastly, each candidate was required to write a short and suc-
cinct account of the late war with England and
France, describing its principal features and its
results.

On all but the last subject, there was little
variety in the number of marks attained; indeed, as all the candidates had been educated by
the same class of schoolmasters, who are called

---

* Orthography is only a subject of examination for very
subordinate offices, it being considered vulgar in China
to spell words according to conventional rules. What we
should call bad spelling is, moreover, looked upon as a proof
of future genius, and a peculiar qualification for the diplomatic service.

" Ko-chings," in contradistinction to a rival sect
called " Kra-mings," there was an extraordinary
resemblance in all their replies, and, as a rule,
wherever one failed, all the rest were found to
be equally at a loss for an answer; but Sia-Lau's
paper on the war was so much the best in point
of composition and accuracy, that he was pronounced the successful competitor, and nomi-
nated to the vacant post from that day year,
subject only to three years' probationary service
without pay. After this, provided he should
have been favourably reported upon by his
superiors as to morals and manners, and could
pass a further examination in ecclesiastical
law, botany, and fortification, he would at
once enter upon his duties as Ninth Paid Assistant.

It will thus be seen at a glance, that the
Chinese Government take all precautions to
ensure the recipients of public money being
equal to their positions, and possessed of every
kind of knowledge likely to be useful to them
in the performance of their official duties.

I transcribe Sia-Lau's paper as a very fair

specimen of the candid and impartial manner
in which History is written in China :—

"In the fifth moon of the tenth year of the
reign of Hien Fung, the wisest and greatest
Emperor that the world has yet known, if we
except the Lord who now reigns, and who is to
all his predecessors, as the sun is to a paper
lantern, it was determined by the Emperor,
whose heart was big, and who loved his people,
to drive out of his dominions, which means
from off the face of the world, all foreign
devils and barbarians, who, by cunning devices
and falsehood, had gained admission into the
land.

"Now, these foreign devils and barbarians
became afraid, and they prepared a humble
petition, praying to be allowed to send deputies
to offer tribute and submission to the Ruler of
the Universe.

"When the Lord of Ten Thousand Years
heard of this audacious request, his anger was
aroused, and he ordered that when these foreigners
came they should be slain.

"It is true, and all men should know, that far

away across a sea which the stupid barbarians
call the Red, because its waters are blue, there
are some islands inhabited by savages, who are
called English, French, American, and other vile
names. These lands are remote and very poor,
so much so that, although under the Imperial
sceptre, the Ruler of the World had taken pity
on them, and allowed their people to dwell in
peace and piggishness. Great was the goodness and the wisdom of the Emperor Hien
Fung !

" But these foreign devils have wicked hearts,
and they came in many ships and with many soldiers, and tried to create fear among the people ;
and three of their great men—the greatest, no
greater than a second-class white-button mandarin*—presumed to approach the shores of the
Empire, even unto the mouth of the Peiho, and
demanded permission to throw themselves at
the foot of the Celestial throne.

---

* Sia-lau places foreign ambassadors rather low in the
table of precedency. The gradations of mandarin rank
are indicated by the little ball or button worn on the
top of the hat, as follows : — 1. Pale red button — 2.
Deep red button—3. Opaque blue—4. Transparent blue—

" The names of these men were Lau-Ghin, an
Englishman, Bar-Glo, a Frenchman, and Yan-
ki-Wad, an American.*   They took with them
Jay-Ho, an English sea-mandarin, with many
ships ; and they said to him, " We would go to
Pekin ; but, see! there are braves on the banks,
and they will kill us ! "

" And Jay-Ho said (Ho was a fool!), 'Come
with me, and fear not, for I will drive them
away ! '

" And Glo and Ghin said, ' Be it so ; ' but
Wad was more cunning, and he surrendered
himself to our braves, who carried him to Pekin
in a wooden cage, and there imprisoned him.

" And Jay-Ho brought 743 ships, each carrying

5. Opaque white—6. Transparent white—with three kinds of
gilt button for inferior classes. The Imperial button is of
scarlet silk.

* There is evidently some blunder here on the part of our
young friend Sia-lau ; Lau-Ghin is supposed to mean Lord
Elgin, who, though he had in person taken the initiative in
inducing the Chinese Government to consent to the admission of representatives at the Court of Pekin, had wisely left
it to others to carry out the practical details of his diplomacy.
He was in England when the first attack on the Peiho Forts
took place.

2317 soldiers, and 419 guns, and he attempted to enter the river; whereupon 100 braves were sent to attack him, and they burned all the ships, and slew all the barbarians, only nine of whom escaped; and among these were Glo and Ghin.

" When the Lord of the Universe heard of these things, he was wroth, and he ordered Wad to be brought before him, and reproached him, scorching the barbarian with his ire; but Wad kotowed, and wept piteously, saying, he was not like those other men, but peaceful and submissive; and that he had a wife and children who would die of hunger if he were killed; and the Emperor took pity and pardoned him, and bade him go back to his country. Merciful was the heart of Hien Fung!

"And before Wad went away, the people derided him; and Lan-see, the Imperial painter, drew a picture of a dog with his tail between his legs, running before the shouting populace; and the dog had not the head of a dog, but the head of a man! and beneath was written, ' This is Yan-ki-Wad!' and when the Emperor saw it, he smiled, like the sun in the heavens ; and he said, 'It is good ! '*

" And the year following, Ghin and Glo, having concocted despatches (which is the term used by the foreign devils for big lies), prevailed upon their people to send more ships and more soldiers, and they came again to the Peiho ; but the Emperor said to his braves, 'Forbid them not to enter, for fain would I see with my own eyes the slaughter of these barbarians.'

" And as they advanced, like a flight of locusts over the land, killing the women and the little children, our braves restrained themselves, in obedience to their Lord and Master, and allowed the red devils to approach, even to the gates of the Celestial City, when the braves could no longer repress their courage, but fell upon them and destroyed them all, excepting a few who were sent as prisoners to Tien-tsin.

* From a marginal note, I conclude that this passage is meant to refer to Mr. Ward, the United States Minister; but though his trip to Pekin was not, as he intended it should be, a triumph over his colleagues, there appears to be some exaggeration in this account of his reception, for the late Emperor of China was, I am sure, too much of a gentleman to laugh at a vulgar caricature of a diplomatic functionary.

" And the Emperor sentenced Ghin to be sawed in half, and Glo to be boiled to death in oil; but they wept sorely at this, and offered large sums in ransom of their lives; and the Emperor, who is merciful as he is wise, took their money and pardoned them, and let them depart; but in order to prevent fresh disturbances, he compelled them to give security; and Lau-Ghin fell upon his knees and offered up his brother as hostage; and Bar-Glo wept aloud, and lamented that he had no brother, but tendered an elderly woman, his nurse; and both these hostages remain imprisoned in Pekin; and all the soldiers, who were not slain, remain imprisoned in Tien-tsin; and they will be put to death with terrible tortures if ever again the barbarians dare to give offence.*

* Captain Harcourt, of H.M.'s 31st Regt., published in the *North China Herald* an extremely interesting account of a journey which he performed from Tien-tsin to Cheefoo, south of the Peiho, a distance inland of above 700 miles. He confirms the opinion of most other recent travellers in the interior of China, that the Treaty is a dead letter, except at the open ports, and that the people are fully impressed with the belief that we were ignominiously defeated in our attempt to reach Pekin. Captain Harcourt says, after reaching

"And this is the History of the War with the Barbarians, under the reign of Hien Fung."

Tey-chow:—"Many Tartars came to see us to-day; their officer was a big, tall fellow, with mandarin hat, with blue button and peacock's feather, under which were two marten or minx tails sewed on red cloth. He appreciated rum immensely, and much admired our revolvers. He was from the Amoor territory, on his way to join San-ko-lin-sin. He had seen plenty of Russians, he said, and on being asked which he liked best, the Russians or ourselves, said, 'There is no difference between you, as you are the same nation, tributary to the Emperor.' We said, 'We are independent of your Emperor.' On which he rejoined, 'What are you obliged to have a house in Pekin for, and why do you send people there to kotow to the Emperor? I know very well that you were in a state of rebellion this year, and marched from Tien-tsin to Pekin, but, once there, you were too glad to be allowed to go back to Tien-tsin again, after making your submission.'"

And again, at Chin-kya-wan:—"In walking about the town, which is evidently prosperous, plenty of trade going on, and good houses and shops, we saw a proclamation by Shinpao (who commanded the Chinese force which lay to S.W. of Pekin, when the Allies were there) saying 'that his appearance with his army before Pekin had induced the allied foreigners to retire to Tien-tsin, and to come to terms, and that now he was going to annihilate the rebels (he has been beaten by them two or three times already), and requesting the people of the country not to be afraid, and to keep quiet.'"

There is, after all, a wonderfully strong likeness throughout the great human family ; and I
could not help feeling, as I stopped one afternoon to watch a number of Tien-tsin children at
their play, how " one touch of nature makes the
whole world kin."

There were boys, wearing pigtails certainly,
but playing at soldiers, or at leapfrog, or at
horses; and little girls, with queer, powdered
faces and elaborate head-dresses, and in trowsers,
dressing and nursing their dolls; and babies—
such quaint, old-fashioned-looking affairs—but
crowing and squealing, and pulling down
mamma's hair, or busily working with their
little fingers at the front opening of mamma's
dress; exactly as boys, girls, and babies would
do in England, and in every other part of the
world that I have ever been in. With ad-
vancing years the likeness wears off; man seems
to diverge more from our common nature as he
grows older, and it is not until he verges on
second childhood that the resemblance breaks
out again, and that the old Chinaman, sunning
himself in his doorway, looks much the same

kind of animal as our old fogey seated in the bow window of his Club. .

An acquaintance of mine was once consulted by a female servant as to which of two suitors she ought to accept. One was an Irishman, who owned two cows; the other was a Scotchman, who owned three : her inclination was rather for the Hibernian lover, as the nicer man, but she could not quite decide for herself.

"Marry the Scotchman," said her master, "for, take my word for it, there is not the difference of a cow between any two men that ever lived."

I really begin to think that, barring climate and a few other local circumstances and artificial influences, there are no varieties worth mentioning in the genus man.

There are some articles of Chinese chow-chow extremely palatable. I don't mean bird's-nests or shark's-fins, tasteless, glutinous substances, reserved as rare luxuries for the wealthy; or even the luscious green sea-slug, which in flavour resembles an oyster fed upon train-oil; but the ordinary food of the well-to-do people, flesh, fish, or fowl, chopped small and stewed or fried with a variety of herbs, really makes very agreeable dishes. As for the poor, they rarely taste animal food, and subsist principally upon messes composed of different farinaceous materials. In the north, even rice is a luxury beyond their reach. I once saw a group of coolies in unmistakable enjoyment of a very strange-looking dish. On inquiring into its nature, I found that it consisted of fried grass-hoppers, garnished with boiled bamboo twigs or stalks.

What would a poor Chinaman do without the bamboo? Independently of its use as food, it provides him with the thatch that covers his house, the mat on which he sleeps, the cup from which he drinks, and the chopsticks with which he eats.

He irrigates his field by means of a bamboo pipe; his harvest is gathered in with a bamboo rake; his grain is sifted through a bamboo sieve, and carried away in a bamboo basket.

The mast of his junk is of bamboo; so is the pole of his cart. He is flogged with a bamboo cane, tortured with bamboo stakes, and finally strangled with a bamboo rope.

————————

Died of sheer exhaustion at Ye-hol, on the 22nd of August, 1861, in the thirtieth year of his age, Hien Fung, Emperor of China.

Among the most hackneyed of common-place quotations which we hear or read daily, there is one, in common-place Latin, which teaches us that we should say none but pretty things of the dead. You have a perfect right to speak the most injurious truths of your neighbour while he lives and can suffer from the effect of your evil report; but, once buried and beyond the reach of calumny, be civil to him, give him credit for every virtue, and confirm each flattering lie inscribed upon his tombstone.

Crowned heads receive, as a rule, so much adulation during their lives, and are so lavishly and constantly bespattered with fulsome praise while they can appreciate or reward it, that there is little left to be said for them after death. A dead lion is not worth a live ass; and a dead lord ranks with a commoner. Courtiers are too busy worshipping the rising planet to waste much time upon the star that has vanished from their hemisphere : *Le roi est mort—Vive le roi!* So I take it, upon the whole, that kings and emperors do not fare so well after death as their subjects; " the evil that *they* do lives after them ;" while commoner people have it " interred with their bones."

It would appear, however, that the Emperor of China takes the precaution of guarding his posthumous character against the neglect or ill-nature of his biographers, by leaving behind him an instrument which contains his own valuation of himself; and that his successor, moreover, makes it a point of honour to endorse this document, and to secure for the deceased monarch as high a title in the records of his dynasty as circumstances will allow. It will be somewhat difficult to place the late Emperor above his father and predecessor, who was canonized as "the Perfect"; but probably there are degrees, even of perfection, in China.

It is just as well that the Emperor Hien Fung did write his own character, for Europeans had very generally conceived a notion that he was a tyrant, a coward, and a liar, and that his gross vices had reduced him to imbecility, and brought him to an untimely grave. We now find, and on no less an authority than his own, that he was, on the contrary, possessed of every virtue that can dignify a monarch, or adorn a man.

In his last decree,* Hien Fung says:—" Already grateful for the disinterested affection with which his late Majesty, canonized as the Perfect, had covered us, as with a canopy, and nourished us, we received the trust he, of his goodness and of his care for the Empire, committed to our keeping, in humble accordance with the commands reiterated to us by the Sainted One,

---

* This document, dated only a few days before the Emperor's death, was promulgated in the *Pekin Gazette* on August 23, 1861, and republished in English in the *North China Herald.*

namely, that we should regard as fixed principles a devout fear of Heaven, the imitation of our ancestors, diligent attention to government, and love for the people, a respectful appreciation of unselfishness, the maintenance of peace, and self-restraint. As soon as we had come to the throne, we commanded our servants to recommend us men of worth and ability; we widened the path of words, so that all our servants, great or small, might set forth each one his opinions; it being our hope that so we might have the larger choice of counsel, and be informed of all things, the feelings of those below not being hidden from us. And from the time of our accession until now, eleven years, we have given daily attention to our more than myriad affairs. Ourself opening and perusing all documents submitted to us, and giving audience to our servants, we have idled not, were it ever so little, a single day."

Unfortunately, the poor Emperor's efforts for the happiness of his people were vain; foreign wars and rebellion prevailed throughout the land.

"Constant reflection upon the suffering of our black-haired people, exposed, time after time, to the flame of war, has scorched us, and worn us early and late. We could neither sleep nor eat in comfort; and thus, at last, our bodily strength has waxed weak from the wound that over-anxiety inflicted on our spirits."

In spite of loss of appetite and low spirits, however, he toiled on at Ye-hol, for his country's good, until at last he was attacked in another quarter.

"Ever since the beginning of this summer, a violent dysentery has set in, long continuance of which has produced such debility, that we had at last too little strength left to rise."

Then, as he felt death approaching, this model monarch sent for his ministers, and commended to their care his son and heir, who, though only six years of age, is, according to his father's evidence,—

"Humane and dutiful, quick and intelligent. He will not fail to respect the charge entrusted to him. Let him straightway ascend the throne and continue the Imperial line." . . .

"Let the princes and ministers who form our *suite* here, and the princes and ministers now in the capital, with pure heart, and in friendly concert, unite to aid him, so that his administration may improve until it attain perfection."

Accordingly, Tsai-Chun ascends the throne, and his first act is the issue of an Imperial manifesto, in which he entirely approves of his late father's choice of a successor,* and proceeds, in a touching strain of filial piety, to tell us,—

"We had been the object of his Majesty the late Emperor's great bounty, than which high heaven is not more infinite. He fed and watched us. And the years of the Sainted One being but just past thirty, as we waited on him in the Palace, our love for him increasing day by day, we hoped that he might count upon a century.

"Last summer it chanced that he was affected

---

* The Emperor of China may select any male member of the Royal Family to succeed him, unless he be of the issue of the legitimate wife and Empress, which is excluded from succession.

with a cough and expectoration, but under medical treatment he recovered, and after the Imperial tour to Ye-hol in the autumn, the person
of the Sainted One was as well and strong as
ever. But the continued disorders of the provinces, occasioned by the pestilence of rebellion,
gave him anxiety by night and by day; and, in
the spring of this year, a cold he had caught
caused his malady to break out afresh, while in
the sixth moon he was attacked by a dysentery, which by degrees greatly reduced his
strength. . . . .

" Then with bitter tears we received his commands, grieving and anxious, trembling and
awe-struck. We hoped that the person of the
Affectionate One might yet be saved, and that
for long we should continue to receive his gracious commands. But after we had in person
been informed of the will of him that regarded
us fondly, his malady attacked him with increasing violence ; bringing him presently to the
last extremity, and on the 17th day in the *yin*
watch (3 to 5 A.M.) he sped upwards upon the
dragon to be a guest on high. We tore the

earth and cried to Heaven, yet reached we not to him with our hand or voice.

" With reverence we call to mind that his late Majesty, during the eleven years that he sat upon the throne, with earnest zeal, with painful solicitude, toiled much and rested little, amid his more than myriad affairs, that on no day did he fail in shewing respect to Heaven, or in following in practice the example of his ancestors. Diligence in his administration of the State and love of his people were his chief consideration. He remitted taxes, or gave time for their collection. He chose men of ability. In everything that concerned the policy of the Empire or the well-being of the people, the Sacred One was ever unceasingly forethoughtful. Of all that have blood and breath there can be none that are not most sincerely afflicted at his death. Our own tears are as of blood. We beat our breast."

Then, after promising to imitate the admirable example of his father in all things, he proceeds to confer the rank of Empress Dowager upon the widowed Empress and upon his mother, excuses his uncles from prostration before him, and orders his minister to invent a title of honour by which the deceased Emperor shall be known to posterity.

All these things excite little interest beyond the precincts of the Imperial dominions—perhaps not very much beyond the walls of the Palace. Yet, the accession of an absolute ruler over three or four hundred millions of human beings should be an event of some importance in the history of this world of ours.

———————

A French General of my acquaintance, who entertains a profound contempt for Eastern diplomacy, had one universal recipe for the management of the Chinese : " *Il n'y qu'un seul moyen, il faut tapper dessus.*"

We have been playing this game in China, off and on, for some years past ; but to *tapper dessus* with effect requires a large military force, and to maintain this costs more money than our interests in that country are worth. We have now knocked a good treaty out of them, but time alone can show whether we can place reliance upon the good faith of an essentially false people. In spite of the pretensions of our diplomatists, every concession made by the Chinese Government has been wrung from them by our soldiers and sailors, and it remains to be seen what will become their attitude when military pressure shall be removed, and ministers and consuls left to their own devices for maintaining or enforcing treaty obligations.

Fortunately, there are among our consuls in the East some men who have acquired a thorough insight into the Chinese character without losing the best qualities of intelligent Englishmen who can be firm without arrogance, conciliatory without truckling, and capable of maintaining their own nation's rights without injustice to the people to which they are accredited. It is, however, always the safest plan in dealing with the Chinese to keep a gun-boat in reserve as your last argument.

I have said before that our treaty was a dead letter in the interior of the country ; but even in some of the ports lately opened to trade

neither the officials nor the people showed themselves well-disposed towards Europeans. At
New-chwang their attitude had been particularly
unfriendly, when a circumstance occurred which
enabled us to assert our right to a better reception.

Mr. Davenport, Consular Interpreter at New-
chwang, unmindful of the fact proverbially befall-
ing those who in others' quarrels interpose, and
more particularly when the quarrel is of a domestic nature, on seeing a Chinaman furiously
beating his wife, interfered in the lady's behalf,
and was immediately set upon by the combatants
and their neighbours, who, armed with bill-
hooks, scythes, and other agricultural implements, attacked the unfortunate interpreter, the
injured wife taking a prominent part in the assault upon her champion. He was left for dead
by the roadside.

On redress being demanded, the mandarin of
the district defended the outrage, and declined to
accede to the Consul's request for the punishment of the offenders.

Mr. Meadows thereupon, feeling that a lesson

was necessary to inculcate respect for the persons of Europeans in this remote part of the country, ordered up a gun-boat, the crew of which was landed, and after repeated refusals to punish the guilty, burnt the principal houses in the village. This .brought the mandarin to reason, and . ever since the people of New-chwang have entertained the greatest regard and respect for us.

Many excellent well-meaning people in England will feel horrified at these harsh measures, and condemn such exercise of power as a barbarism : they, in like manner, disapproved of the execution of the " poor sepoys," who butchered our women and children in India, and of the destruction of Yuen-ming-Yuen in retaliation for the murder by torture of English prisoners. But, nevertheless, there are occasions when such things are necessary—when severity becomes a virtue and even cruelty a mercy.

Mr. Davenport recovered from his wounds. The woman, on being reproached for having turned upon her protector, justified her conduct by asserting that he, in coming to her assistance,

was guilty of an unpardonable insult as imply-
ing a claim upon her, and that if her husband
chose to beat or to kill her, what business was
that of any one else? Was she not ever his own?

I beg to commend this laudable sentiment to
the attention of European wives.

When the allied armies of England and
France marched into Taku, the Emperor of
China marched out of Pekin, and took up his
residence at his shooting-lodge at Ye-hol in
Mongolia.

This step had been urged upon him by his
general, San-ko-lin-sin, who represented the possibility of the Allies reaching Pekin, and making
the Emperor a prisoner in his capital, whereas,
if he retired, then the general would "be at
liberty to choose his own time, and mode of
attack, and would, without doubt, sweep the vile
brood from off the earth." *

The ministers, however, and many of the high

* This, and the subsequent quotations, are taken from the
original dispatches found at *Yuen-ming-Yuen*, and translated
by a member of the British Legation.

officers of state joined in opposing this project, in a tone of independence which is apt to stagger one's belief in his Celestial Majesty's absolutism. No European ministry, except our own, would presume to address their sovereign in so fearless and plain-spoken a manner.

"Your minister has heard, with the greatest surprise and alarm," says Tsuan-Kin, "that in consequence of the failure of the attempt to bring the Barbarians to terms, Your Majesty had resolved on making a tour to Ye-hol. At such a moment as this, when the capital is the sovereign's only proper place of residence, is it proper suddenly to propose a hunting-tour? This sudden departure, without any apparent reason, although called a hunting-tour, will bear the aspect of a flight. . . . In a period of public distress, the man of heroic character is prepared to die at his post."

This is language which only under extraordinary circumstances a responsible adviser of the Crown would venture to address to a constitutional monarch.

Now and then a compliment is judiciously

introduced to put the Emperor into good-
humour, but, in some of these, the irony is
stronger than the flattery.

"Your ministers have to-day read the
vermillion decree, stating that the arrangements for Your Majesty's proposed hunting
expedition are to serve as preparation for
taking the field in person. . . . . They
admire the awe-inspiring demeanour and the
strategic ability thus displayed. *But the
common people are extremely slow of comprehension; they easily suspect, and with difficulty
appreciate;* they will say that the Barbarians
are to the south-eastward of the capital, and
that the sudden change from a hunting-tour
to taking the field in person should induce Your
Majesty rather to proceed to Tunchow for the
support of San-ko-lin-sin; that the taking up a
post to the northward of the capital *would be
desertion from the seat of war;* that what in
name was a campaign was in reality a hunting-
tour. . . . . . Your Majesty is familiar
with the maxim, that the prince is bound to
sacrifice himself for his country."

Ai-jin, a censor, reminds his Majesty of the fate of Kia Tsing, of the Ming dynasty (A.D. 1457), who, having gone out shooting to escape taking part in war, "narrowly missed having to pass the remainder of his days in retirement in the south of the country" (*i. e.* deposition); and concludes by saying, "that a puff of breath is now sufficient to decide the balance on which hangs the loss or preservation of the succession of your ancestors and the repose of the tutelary gods" (in other words, the fate of the dynasty).

Tsoo-sang-yung, Governor of the Noo-kwang provinces, condemns the flight after its accomplishment in yet stronger terms :—

"The effect will be like a convulsion of nature, and the mischief irreparable. In what light does Your Majesty regard your people? in what light the shrines of your ancestors, or the altars of the tutelary gods? Will you cast away the inheritance of your ancestors like a damaged shoe?"

Then, in the terms of an advertisement in the second column of the *Times*, he adds : "I beseech

Your Majesty to return without delay to your palace, in order that the people's minds may be re-assured."

This gentleman holds us very cheap; and thinks that, considering the spirit of the people, women and children even being determined to fight to the last, "the enrolment of volunteers in the Tien-tsin district would suffice to put down the Barbarians, who do not exceed a few thousands, and a considerable portion of whose force consists of hired traitorous Chinese;" * adding that "if the outside Barbarians are to be controlled, it is certain that peace could not be accorded before they have been defeated in battle. His late Imperial Majesty, in his testament, speaks with shame and contrition of the peace with the English Barbarians."

However, warning and remonstrance were vain; the Emperor remained at Ye-hol, and, although the representatives of England and France continued to be amused with assurances

* This, probably, refers to the Commissariat Coolie Corps, which was raised in the south, and as transport animals, did excellent service throughout the campaign.

of his speedy return to the capital, they waited in vain. When he did make his entry, it was in his coffin, and in company with his young son and successor.

This boy had been placed in charge of a Council of Regency, composed of the worst and most illiberal of the late Emperor's advisers; and Prince Kung, who had read modern European history to some effect, and is said to be an ardent admirer of Louis Napoleon, determined to withdraw his young nephew from the obnoxious influences with which he was surrounded. The return to Pekin offered the desired opportunity for a *coup d'état*, which could not have been better planned or executed in Paris.

About ten miles from Pekin the royal procession was met by a guard of honour, who handcuffed the Council of Eight on a charge of treason, and carried them as prisoners into the capital.

A very short trial sufficed to decide their fate. Su-shun appears to have been the arch-offender. Independently of his having exercised his power

over his late master to the detriment of the
State, he had, while finance minister, depreciated the currency of Pekin to such an extent
that many thousands were ruined, and all the
trading classes suffered heavy losses. At the
same time, he was instrumental in raising the
price of grain, and thus incurred the odium of
the populace. He was sentenced to decapitation, and underwent his fate with due submission. Borne in his chair to a square in the
centre of one of the main streets of Pekin, he
stepped out and was greeted with the yells
and howls of the assembled multitude. A high
officer of justice then approached him, read the
sentence, made the mark of a red cross upon
his forehead, and handed him over to the executioners. One of them drew his neck forward
by means of his pigtail; another drew his body
backward; and the head fell at one blow.

Twan-hwa, Prince of Ching, elder brother of
Su-shun and chief minister of police, and Tsai
Yuen, Prince of E, half brothers of the late
Emperor, were likewise condemned to death, but
out of consideration for their families, merci-

fully permitted to strangle themselves in prison silken ropes of Imperial yellow being provided for the purpose at the public expense. Kinshau, uncle-in-law to the late Emperor, Mu-jin, minister of war, and several others, were banished to the colonies; and Prince Kung, having thus removed all obstacles, assumed the regency in concert with the Empress-mother, who is said to be a remarkably strong-minded female, and extremely favourable to European intercourse.

We are not used to such summary measures in England. What would be thought of Lord Derby if, some fine day, having concerted his plans with the Duke of Cambridge and Mr. Disraeli, he sent Lords Palmerston and Russell to the Tower, with permission to hang themselves, executed Mr. Gladstone in Charing Cross, and sentenced the other ministers of the Crown to penal servitude for life? But it is not, after all, so very long since things almost as outrageous were done in England, and even in the present day there are civilized countries in Europe where a similar course might take place

T

without creating much surprise, provided always that the author of the *coup d'état* were perfectly successful.

The death of the Emperor of China so far promised to afford the prospect of more friendly relations, that the English and French representatives agreed to a reduction of the military force in the North. We had hoped that the entire Army of Occupation would have been dispensed with,* but for this it appears the political atmosphere was not yet clear enough. Indeed, it may be doubted whether Pekin will, for many years to come, be a safe or desirable residence for foreign ministers, more particularly during the long winter, when they are completely cut off from communication with the outer world, without some military protection. Probably, the difficulty will ere long be met by the Legations being removed to Shanghae during the winter months.

* Had the *coup d'état* at Pekin occurred earlier in the year, Mr. Bruce, it is said, would have consented to the withdrawal of the entire force from Tien-tsin.

The poor French soldiers, who are not accustomed to do garrison duty out of their own country (their few colonies, with exception of Algeria, being garrisoned by marines), broke out in frantic exclamations of delight when the order for their relief, by a battalion of *infanterie de la marine*, arrived. There was, it is true, a rumour of probable detention on the homeward voyage in Cochin-China; but the French are not prone to indulge in gloomy forebodings, and their vivid imaginations carried them straightway into the vineyards, the cafés, and the theatres of their beloved France.

Our men, of course, took the change coolly. They had grumbled at everything hitherto, and now began to think that they might as well have stayed another winter. I heard some of them complain sadly that their good living was over.*

* The Tien-tsin markets will be long and gratefully remembered by the British soldier. Two corporals of different corps, catering for their respective messes, were overheard comparing notes : "Ah," said one of them, in a patronizing tone, as he surveyed his comrade's purchases, "your mess goes in for solids, and I don't object myself to a good roast sirloin or a joint of lamb now and then ; but our fellows are

Nothing could be more satisfactory than the relations which had existed between the two armies. The *entente cordiale* was as perfect as in Europe. The English soldier had a calm, good-natured contempt for the Frenchman; the French soldier ridiculed and rather hated the Englishman. A river, little wider than the Serpentine in Hyde Park, was the only barrier between them; but the east and west banks of the Peiho were as distinct in their nationalities as England and France. There was never the slightest approach to intimacy, and they were always the best of friends.

The generals and superior officers of the two armies met occasionally and interchanged courtesies and dinners. Between the juniors there was little communication. In spite of Burlington House, the British subaltern has not made any sensible progress in the French language, nor does English appear to be much cultivated by our allies. Besides this serious obstacle, the

all for *entrées*. Now, to-day we had hare-soup, stewed pheasant, and roast grouse; what our cook breaks down in is the pastry."

habits and pursuits of English and French regimental officers are so different as to render mutual intercourse little agreeable to either. While the former would be cricketing, rowing, shooting, or racing, the latter would lounge about the streets, smoking their cigarettes, or sit indoors playing dominoes and *ecarté*. Now and then, a French officer might be seen, in uniform, astride a pony, with a fowling-piece slung across his back, returning from *la chasse*, with a hare or a fox dangling from his saddle-bows (*fox-shooting* was rather a favourite sport among our friends across the river); and one captain, of British predilections, used to join our paper hunts, carrying, and occasionally blowing, a French horn, and go at everything in his way with an admirable disregard for his neck, simply, as he assured us, from a love of *le sport*, which he accounted for by the fact of his mother having been born in the Highlands of Scotland. But these were exceptions; as a general rule, the officers of the two armies did not fraternize, and were accordingly on the best of terms.

I had the good fortune to be intimately acquainted with several officers of the French Staff, and in no service can more accomplished or better-bred men be found; but it was evident that there is a strong line of demarcation between these, the educated classes, and the soldiers who, sprung from a different grade of society, have raised themselves, by good or long service, to the rank of officers; these form the great majority, and are apt to look upon their more favoured comrades as an unjustly privileged class.*

That unanimity and good feeling which, as a rule, prevails in an English regiment, is not found in the French service, where military rank is also much more asserted in private life than with us.

The happy intercourse of an English mess-table, where all classes of officers, from the colonel to the ensign, meet upon terms of per-

* There is also considerable jealousy between the French army and navy; the officers of the latter being considered " aristocrats." If superior accomplishments and polished manners be aristocratic vices, then, judging from my somewhat limited experience, I should say that the reproach is deserved.

ect social equality, restrained only by the ordinary laws of courtesy and good breeding, would be simply impossible with our allies.

———

What would our financial reformers have said could they have been present when, on the removal of the cavalry, military train, and artillery, from Tien-tsin, a general sale of horses, waggons, and camp equipage, took place?—when troop horses, which had probably cost £150 each by the time they were landed in the North, were sold, to avoid the expense of their conveyance back, for ten or twenty dollars; and scores upon scores of waggons, carefully manufactured, regardless of price, in the Carriage Department at Woolwich, were broken up for fire-wood?

Mr. Bright is quite right. War is about the most expensive game that nations can play at; and if we could but induce all mankind to abstain from violence, and covetousness, and oppression, and fraud, and to hate glory, and to love one another, what money the public might save, and what a sad thing it would be for poor soldiers and sailors who hope for promotion!

The sale by auction of a thousand horses was an event of considerable importance in Tien-tsin, and gave rise to some amusing scenes.

Among the troopers of Fane's Horse were some very vicious ones. They were manageable enough while with their Sikh riders or Syces; but when they fell into the hands of English or French soldiers, or of Chinamen, their true character would break out. One unfortunate French officer, having paid five pounds for a beautiful little Gulf Arab, found his purchase so utterly unmanageable that he finally offered a Chinaman a dollar for removing the horse from his premises. Another horse was no sooner in possession of his new owner than he positively refused to allow any white man to enter his stable; and the groom had, at last, to resort to the device of blackening his face and wearing a red turban, as the only means of approaching his charge. It was also reported that a powerful Cape horse had been seen scampering through the streets, with head and tail erect, and carrying his owner, a fat Chinaman, between his teeth.

The men of infantry regiments seemed to have been converted into cavalry, and might be seen tearing over the plains in all directions, with that utter disregard for every law of horse-manship and humanity peculiar to the British soldier. Mounted sailors would suddenly dash out of the most unexpected places, at a furious pace, and nearly run you down, replying to your remonstrances with a blow from a small spar over the horse's head, and an assurance, accompanied by strong oaths and vigorous hauling at the tiller ropes, that "the devil won't answer the helm!"

English shopkeepers and their assistants, too, deserted their business for a time, and, in top-boots and breeches, their bodies bent forward after the fashion of jockeys, and their toes turned out after a fashion of their own, went into a desperate course of training for some future Derby.

It may be some consolation to English tax-payers to know that, if the sale of public horses in Tien-tsin lost them some hundred thousand pounds, their countrymen in a remote corner of the other end of the world got some little amusement out of the sacrifice.

———

"In leaving e'en the most unpleasant people
And places, one keeps looking at the steeple."

There were no steeples in Tien-tsin, or I suppose I might have turned a last lingering look upon them as a French gun-boat bore me past its muddy banks, on my homeward way.

Byron is quite right; I should not think well of the man who could leave a place in which he has passed even a few weeks without some sort of regret for something or other that he had left behind. The homeward-bound can afford to be generous and good-natured; and so, as we steamed away, I forgot all disagreeable smells, sights, and sounds; forgave all my enemies from my heart; pitied the poor fellows who remained; and thought that, perhaps, after all, there might be worse places than Tien-tsin, though, on calm reflection, I most sincerely hope that my experience may never justify such an opinion.

APPENDIX. I.

I am indebted to Mr. John Veitch for the following memorandum on the vegetation of the districts through which we passed in visiting Fusi-jama.

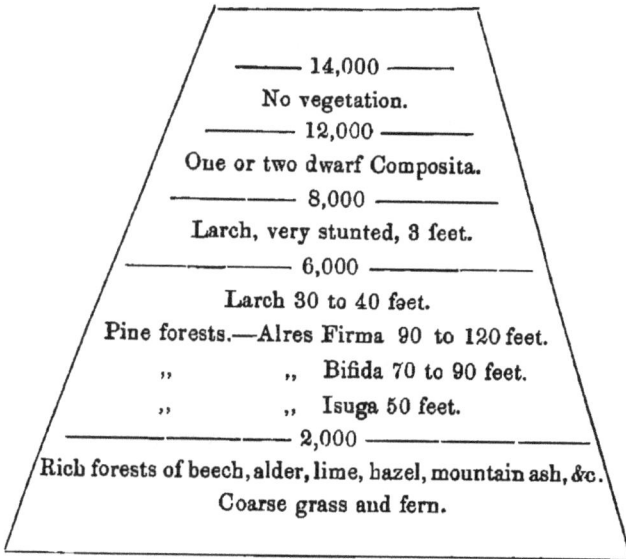

——— 14,000 ———
No vegetation.
——— 12,000 ———
One or two dwarf Composita.
——— 8,000 ———
Larch, very stunted, 3 feet.
——— 6,000 ———
Larch 30 to 40 feet.
Pine forests.—Alres Firma 90 to 120 feet.
,,   ,,   Bifida 70 to 90 feet.
,,   ,,   Isuga 50 feet.
——— 2,000 ———
Rich forests of beech, alder, lime, hazel, mountain ash, &c.
Coarse grass and fern.

Vegetation on the Mountain.

A few of the most striking plants met with during the excursion :—

Alres Leptolepis.

,,   Firma.

,,   Bifida.

,,   Isuga.

Acer (Maple)—many species.

Adiantum—sp. nova (Mount Hakoni).

Alnus Glutinosa.

Aralia Edulis.

    ,,   Sieboldi.

Aucuba Japonica.

    ,,   ,,   folius variegatus.

Asplenium fontanum.

Azaleas—splendid bushes, very common.

Bambusa Metake.

    ,,   ,,   folius variegatus.

Benthamia Japonica.

Berberis Japonica.

Brossoentia Papyrifera.

Buddlea sp.

Camellia Japonica—immense trees.

Cephalotaxus—sp. nova (Mount Hakoni).

    ,,   ,,   (Fusi-jama).

Castanea Sesca.

Chamerops Excelsa.

Citrus Japonica.

Clematis—two or three species.

Corylus Avellana.

Cryptomeria Japonica (some 160 feet high, and 17 inches in circumference).

Cycas revoluta.

Daphne Japonica, folius variegatus.

Deutzia Scabra.

Diervillea—two or three sp.

Erybotria Japonica.

Euonymus Japonica.

Fagus Sylvatica.

Forsythia Suspensa.

Funkia—two variegated varieties.

Gardenia Florida.

    ,,   Radicans.

Hibiscus mutabilis.

Hydrangea Japonica.

    ,,   Bracteuta.

    ,,   Nirta.

Illicum floridanum.

    ,,   Religiosum.

Ilex—sp. unknown.

Iris—very commonly planted on the ridges of the thatched cottages.

Juniperus Rigida.

Laurus Cinnamomea.

Lilium Callosium.

Magnolia sp. (Fusi-jama).

Musa Paradisiaca—the Plantain.

Nerium Japonicum.

Orontium Japonicum.

Paulonia Imperialis.

Pernettya—sp. nova—covered with pink berries (Fusi-jama).

Pinus Massoniana.

    ,,   Parviflora.

Pittosporum Tobira.

Podocarpus Macrophylla.

Pomceana Regia.

Quercus Cuspidata.

    ,,   Glabra.

Retinospora Obtusa.

    ,,   Pisifera.

Rubrus—sp. unknown (Fusi-jama).

Spirea Thunbergii.

   ,,   sp. unknown (Fusi-jama).

Sciadopitys Verticillata.

Thea Bohea.

Thuyopsis Dolobrata.

Thuya Pendula.

   ,,   Orientalis.

Weigelia Rosea.

Wisteria Sinensis.

Woodwardia Japonica.

The principal Agricultural Crops, Vegetables, &c., &c., are—

Rice—one species, grown on irrigated, and two on dry, ground.

Millet—one species grown in fields similar to corn-fields, three to four feet high; and two species, transplanted in single lines, five to six feet high.

Sweet Potato (Dioscorea Balatas).

Egg Plant (Solanum Esculentum).

Indian Corn.

Beans, several kinds of, dwarf and running.

Peas, a dwarf kind, growing in fields.

Carrots, turnips, onions, pumpkins, &c., &c., grown by all cottagers.

Tobacco and cotton—in small quantities only in these districts.

Fruits.

Cherries, chestnuts, figs, grapes, oranges, pears, peaches, plums, walnuts, and two or three kinds of melons.

With exception of the grapes, which are delicious, none of these have as fine a flavour as European fruits.

APPENDIX II.

For the benefit of future Fusi-jama tourists, I subjoin our march route :—

	Rees.	
Sinagawa to Kavasaki	2	8
Kavasaki to Kanagawa	2	8
Kanagawa to Hato-gaja	1	9
Hato-gaja to Totsoka	2	9
Totsoka to Fusi-sawa	1	30
Fusi-sawa to Hilatska	3	18
Hilatska to Ooisa	0	26
Ooisa to Odawara	4	0
Odawara to Yu-moto	1	10
Yu-moto to Hakoni	2	18
Hakoni to Missima	3	28
Missima to Yusi-wara	6	6
Yusi-wara to Omia	2	0
Omia to Muri-jama	2	0
Muri-jama to Hatchi-mondo	1	18
Hatchi-mondo to Ninth Hut	5	0
Ninth Hut to Summit	2	18
	44	26

Equal to 123 English miles.

Woodfall and Kinder, Printers, Angel Court, Skinner Street, London.